FROM SUPERFICIAL TO SIGNIFICANT

DAVID CHADWICK

HARVEST HOUSE PUBLISHERS
EUGENE, OREGON

FROM SUPERFICIAL TO SIGNIFICANT
Copyright © David Chadwick
Published by Harvest House Publishers
Eugene, Oregon 97402
www.harvesthousepublishers.com

ISBN 978-0-7369-6731-0 (pbk.)
ISBN 978-0-7369-6732-7 (eBook)

Library of Congress Cataloging-in-Publication Data
Names: Chadwick, David (David Egbert), author.
Title: From superficial to significant / David Chadwick.
Description: Eugene, Oregon : Harvest House Publishers, 2017. | Includes
    bibliographical references.
Identifiers: LCCN 2016050273 (print) | LCCN 2017006252 (ebook) | ISBN
    9780736967310 (pbk.) | ISBN 9780736967327 (ebook)
Subjects: LCSH: Success—Religious aspects—Christianity. | Sports—Religious
    aspects—Christianity. | Jesus Christ—Example.
Classification: LCC BV4598.3 .C43 2017 (print) | LCC BV4598.3 (ebook) | DDC
    248.4—dc23
LC record available at https://lccn.loc.gov/2016050273

Printed in the United States of America

17 18 19 20 21 22 23 24 25 / BP-SK / 10 9 8 7 6 5 4 3 2 1

DEDICATION

I wrote this book to help future generations know what it means to faithfully follow Jesus. Therefore, I dedicate this book to the future generations that flow from my love for my beloved wife, Marilynn, and own personal family tree.

To my firstborn daughter, Bethany, and your faithful husband Ryan, I dedicate this book. May these ten truths remind you of my life's passions and priorities. I pray you'll pass them on to your children Anna Grace, Caleb, Emily, and Joshua (and any others our Lord may choose to give you!). I pray they will similarly become the passion of their hearts and then pass them on to their kids. It will be the best way they can remember and honor their Pappy.

To my firstborn son, David, and his beautiful wife Jessie, I dedicate this book. May these ten truths help you personally grow closer to Jesus. May they assist you to disciple your kids and my grandkids yet to come. As you pass them on to your kids and mentor them faithfully, may they have in their hearts the legacy of faith Pappy wanted them to possess for eternity. I pray they will pass them on to their kids as well.

To my second-born son, Michael, and your bride-to-be, may these ten truths become the foundation of your faith. May they help you and your wife draw closer to Jesus. May you use them to plant seeds of faith into the hearts of your kids and my grandkids. As you then teach and mentor them with these truths about following Jesus, may they always remember what really impassioned and motivated their Pappy. And may they pass them on to their kids as well.

To my children and their spouses, please plant these truths into your hearts. Please plant them in my grandkids' hearts as well. My prayer is they will do the same with their kids, my great grandkids.

When this is done, I will have truly made disciples, who have made disciples, who will make disciples, who will make disciples of all the nations.

I give thanks to God for all the joy you've brought to my life.

To all of you, I dedicate this book.

ACKNOWLEDGMENTS

Writing a book can be a challenging process. There are writings, deadlines, rewritings, and more deadlines. Sometimes you wonder if you'll ever complete the project. It's not for the fainthearted.

Yet with every writing challenge set before me with this book, I never sighed with resignation and said to myself, "I have to write this book." Instead, I always inwardly reflected with excitement, "I get to write this book."

It's a distinct privilege to write a book. I never want to take it for granted.

But no book mysteriously and suddenly appears out of nowhere. It not only takes long, arduous, and intense hours of thoughtful reflection and writing, but it also takes many different people who work and cheer behind the scenes to help the book become a finished product.

That's certainly the case with this book. Therefore, I want to acknowledge all those who helped make this book possible.

First, to my beloved Marilynn, thank you for almost four decades of faithful love and friendship. On those days when I didn't think I could keep pursuing deadlines amidst my various other responsibilities, you kept reminding me I could do it. You believed in me. With constant encouragement, you kept saying, "You get to write a book. How exciting!"

To my good friends Christina Wilking and Kathleen McClendon, thank you for working with me. You constantly printed out my edited chapters so I could rewrite them and meet deadlines. Without your help, the book could have not been finished. I'm very grateful to you both.

To the staff of Forest Hill Church, thank you for being so gifted and passionate about your call. If you didn't do your job so well, I wouldn't be able to take time away to write. Remarkably, I'd always return and find out everything was going just fine. You didn't miss a beat in my absence. Thank you.

To the elders of Forest Hill Church, thank you for giving me the time to write. You believed I could. You encouraged me to do so. Thank you.

To all the people at Forest Hill Church, thank you for years of believing in and following me. You've been a pleasure to lead and oversee. My leadership and preaching have desired, above all else, to move you from superficiality to significance. I've been overjoyed to see many of you do so.

To my friends at Harvest House, I sincerely appreciate all you've done to make this book possible. From sales, to the design of the cover, to just believing in me, I'm very grateful.

And finally, to my friend and editor Steve Miller, thank you for your careful corrections and simple suggestions that made the book better and better. As always, if this book is good, it's mostly because of you. Thank you very much.

I got to write a book! It's been a pleasure to do so.

Thanks to all who helped make it happen.

CONTENTS

THE IMITATION GAME

Right after I had graduated from high school, I attended a Fellowship of Christian Athletes Conference in Black Mountain, North Carolina. I had just signed a basketball scholarship to play at one of the nation's most heralded basketball schools—the University of North Carolina. I thought I was pretty good. In fact, I had a bit of a swagger about my basketball ability and acumen.

At the end of one of the sessions at the conference, word got out that there would be a basketball game later that afternoon. Anyone who was good was invited to come. Of course I showed up, ready to show off my ability.

The teams were divided up. I was fortunate to be chosen among the first ten who were present.

During the first scrimmage, I was paired against an NBA player who had been selected to the all-star team the year before. He was big, strong, fast, and skilled. He guarded me and I guarded him. I was excited to see how I would fare against him.

At the end of the scrimmage, I was exhausted and had been beaten to a pulp. He was so good defensively that I didn't even score a point. On the offensive end, I couldn't stop him from doing what he wanted. He scored on me at will. My swagger soon changed to humiliation. I walked off the court with my head bowed, totally dejected.

I went to him after the game and humbly asked, "Would you teach me how to play basketball? I thought I knew how to play the game, but I don't. You know how to play basketball. Please teach me."

He graciously and gladly agreed to help me. For the rest of the week, he met with me several times and gave me tips on how to play the game. Over and over again, he'd said, "Just watch what I do and then do it. Copy my moves. Play as I play. Just do that and you'll become a better player."

I did exactly as he suggested. I tried to imitate him in every detail. Sometimes I even found myself copying his facial expressions. As a result, I became significantly better. Imitation is indeed the greatest form of flattery.

I played the imitation game.

Jesus did the same thing with his potential disciples. He said to them, "Follow me." Never did he suggest that Christians stop at simply believing in him to possess eternal life. Yes, eternal life is an invaluable gift. Eternal security is extremely important to understand. But Christians were never intended to stop there. Jesus wanted so much more from his followers.

That's why Jesus said, "Follow me."

Jesus practiced what's commonly called a peripatetic teaching style. This style of teaching involves a teacher who says to his students, "Do what I do. Act as I act. Practice what I practice. Copy how I live. And if you have any questions along the way, ask them and I will answer all of them."

After this training, the teacher then sets his followers free to live as he lived. But he also demands that they find others whom they can teach what they've learned from him. The pupils eventually become teachers to others, who then become teachers to others, who keep passing on these truths for generations to come.

That was Jesus' model. That is still his plan and strategy today.

Therefore, the questions all Christians need to ask themselves are these: Am I faithfully following Jesus? Am I living as he lived? Am I doing what he did? Am I speaking as he spoke? Am I loving as he loved? Am I believing as he believed? Am I copying how he lived? Am I serving as he served? Am I mentoring as he mentored? Is my life imitating his?

If not, can someone really say he is faithfully following Jesus? Is he a true disciple of Jesus?

The intention of this book is to give you ten fundamentals of the Christian faith that Jesus repeatedly practiced. I believe they are at the heart of what it means to follow Jesus. When imitated, you will be faithfully following him. And, you will then be able to mentor others on how to be followers of Jesus.

I hope these fundamentals will be useful to you. I pray you will be able to use them to mentor others.

I'm convinced the kingdom of God is advanced when these ten fundamentals are rightly learned and practiced. Jesus is glorified. Non-Christians notice the difference between your life and theirs. They are drawn to Jesus. They hunger for the life you have in Jesus and desire to follow him as well.

You are then truly following Jesus.

You are great in God's sight.

And you have moved from pursuing the superficial trinkets of this world to the significant treasures of eternity.

CHAPTER 1

THE GREAT EXCHANGE

How does someone become great in the eyes of God and move from superficiality to significance? It begins with what some theologians call "The Great Exchange." What does that mean? How does it apply to being great in God's sight?

Let me begin with this illustration. I love baseball. I know some think it's slow and boring. I don't. Since I was a little kid, I've loved baseball. Perhaps it's because I vividly remember something special that happened when I was around ten years old. My dad came home one evening and asked me if I wanted to go with him to the Charlotte Hornets' baseball game. Back in the '50s, Charlotte had a minor league baseball team called the Hornets.

I was excited. I'd never been to a baseball game with my dad until this moment. He was a busy pastor overseeing a growing church. He would often leave early in the morning and come home late at night. Now he was asking me to spend some time with him. (This moment always reminds me that kids spell love T-I-M-E.)

It was not the last time Dad and I attended a baseball game together. Dad had experienced an epiphany. He realized he needed to spend more time with all his kids. He knew he wouldn't get a second chance with us.

Dad also knew how much I loved sports. He did as well. So he found a natural sports connection we both enjoyed: baseball. We always sat in the same seats—ten rows up on the first-base side. At the end of the sixth inning we always got a snow cone—I got orange and he got grape. At the end of the seventh, he'd ask if I wanted to go home. Even if the game was a blowout, I always declined. Inwardly, I cherished every second (and inning) with him.

I am certain that these special moments with Dad are why I love baseball today. Besides thinking it's a pretty cool, engaging, thoughtful, strategic sport, it reminds me of times with Dad.

A Theological Lesson from Baseball

One of the most interesting dates in the major league baseball season is July 31. Why? It's the final day a team can make a trade. It's called the "trading deadline." On that day, at 4:00 in the afternoon, all baseball teams must have completed all their trades.

You may be wondering what does the trading deadline in baseball have to do with a theological understanding of the Great Exchange? A lot. In the same way that baseball teams trade one player for another, in the Christian faith, God has made a huge, life-changing, eternal trade with humanity.

What is it? God has said to everyone, "Tell you what. I'll accept your gross, selfish, treacherous, stained, ego-driven, prideful sinfulness, and in return, you can receive my perfect, sinless righteousness. It's a straight-up trade, no strings attached. Here it is. What do you think? Will you accept it?"

The Bad News

Let's think about it for a moment. The gospel of Jesus Christ begins with the bad news: our lost, sinful condition. We've wandered far from God. We've broken his moral law over and over again. We've committed high treason against the holy, perfect God of the universe. We are guilty of sinful rebellion and deserve eternal separation from the one who created us. There's no ability within us to merit God's approval. We could work from now until the end of our lives, but we'll never be good enough or righteous in his sight.

God demands perfection. He is perfect. Uh-oh! That's a problem. We can never be perfect. It's impossible. We have a selfish, rebellious condition consuming our hearts. We're doomed. It's hopeless. We deserve death for our selfishness and rebellion.

When you examine the Scriptures, you see that we don't have much hope for a relationship with God in our pre-Christ condition. For example, in Romans 5:6-11, look closely at some of the words Paul uses to describe people who have not yet made "the trade": sinner, ungodly, and enemies. It's not very flattering, is it? In Luke 15, Jesus consistently calls us "lost"—a lost sheep, a lost coin, and a lost son.

As one of my friends once said, "The bad news is much worse than you could possibly think or imagine." It is.

But God loves us. He loves this world. Therefore, he entered into it as a sinless human. He lived the perfect, righteous life we can't live. Then he took the penalty of our sin upon himself—something he didn't deserve. He died in our place on the cross—something he didn't deserve. He was raised from the dead, which proved his sacrifice worthy to the Father for the forgiveness of our sin.

That brings me to the second part of my friend's observation that the bad news is much worse than you could possibly think or imagine. He followed that with this statement: "But always remember that the good news is much better than you think."

God entered the human condition; came to sinful, unworthy, rebellious sinners like you and me; and offered us a free gift and trade. By grace, not because of our merit, he trades his perfect righteousness in exchange for our grievous sin.

Second Corinthians 5:21 sums up this astounding trade: "For our sake he made him to be sin who knew no sin so that in him we might become the righteousness of God." All we must do is accept the trade.

It's the most one-sided trade in the history of the world. God trades his perfect righteousness for our damned depravity. It's a straight-up deal. There are no cash considerations. There are no future draft picks involved. There are no players to be named later. Who would be silly enough to turn down this amazingly one-sided deal?

Many call it the Great Exchange. I love to call it the Great Trade.

When it's a done deal through the cross of Christ, it's the first step in being "great" in God's sight. Because of Jesus' death, God now looks into our hearts and sees his Son's absolute, perfect righteousness. We'd be absolutely stupid to turn it down!

A Deeper Dive

Let's analyze the trade more closely by examining the bad news more deeply. You need to begin by knowing what exactly you are trading away.

In my experience, it's very hard for people to admit the bad news. For some, it's a stumbling block. They say, "Hey, I'm a good guy." For others, the idea of a Galilean carpenter dying on a cross so I can be forgiven is offensive.

I've quit trying to argue with people about this. Usually I try to take them to the Ten Commandments as God's perfect moral standard. I carefully go through each one and then ask them if they've broken any. It's obvious they have. Sometimes the moral Law will then convict their hearts. They see their utter depravity, selfishness, and need for a Savior.

Often, however, I receive blank stares. It's as if there are blinders over the eyes of their souls. I've come to understand that until the Holy Spirit convicts people's hearts of the bad news, they will never make the trade and see its incredible, eternal value.

But when people *do* become convicted of their sin, they begin to hate sin. They despise what it has done to their soul and how it's separated them from their Creator. They hate what it's done to their own lives. They hate what it's done to their families. They hate what it's done to former relationships. They hate what it's done to God's world.

The good news is medicine for the sin-sick soul. It proclaims not only that forgiveness is possible, but also that God wants to make a trade: his perfection for their sin.

The Bible calls it moving from darkness to light (1 Peter 2:9). It's commonly called conversion as well. It's being on one team, then suddenly being traded and becoming a member of another. It's going from the home team to your most vicious rival, the team you most wanted to beat. Loyalties suddenly change.

A Personal Confession

You've heard it said that confession is good for the soul. Okay, here goes. Even though I love baseball, basketball has always been my first love in sports. I had the privilege of being a scholarship basketball player at the University of North Carolina. My basketball loyalties run "baby blue," UNC's well-known primary color.

Duke University is Carolina's archrival in basketball. Over decades, they have regularly been featured as two of the best teams in the country. When they play each other, it's a national event. It's a fierce rivalry.

A friend of mine was the producer for a TV program for North Carolina public television. One time, his guest was Mike Krzyzewski, the legendary Duke head basketball coach. My friend told Coach K (as he is affectionately known) about me. More specifically, he told him about my total devotion to the University of North Carolina.

Within a week, I received a package in the mail from the Sports Information Department at Duke University. In it was a picture of Coach K, kneeling on the sidelines, coaching in a game. On the picture, he had scribbled, "To David Chadwick, good player, wrong team!" He signed his name under it.

But here's what a lot of people don't know and where my confession enters the picture. Okay, here goes. This is hard. Psychologists say, "Admitting the feeling is the beginning of healing." I'm now ready.

When I was a kid, through my junior year in high school, I was an avid, rabid Duke basketball fan. There. I feel better already. It's true.

Dad attended Duke Divinity School. Yes, my Dad attended Duke. He's gone to be with the Lord. But I have his Duke diploma in my garage today (not hanging anywhere, mind you, just in my garage!).

Dad was a huge Duke fan as I was growing up. Therefore, so was I. I rooted for them in everything, especially in basketball. Vividly, I remember their great 1960s teams, especially during my junior year when they almost won the NCAA championship, losing to Texas Western (now known as UTEP, the University of Texas at El Paso) in the final game. I remember being very sad that day, learning my beloved Blue Devils had lost the national championship game.

As I personally became more successful in basketball at Orlando Boone High School in Orlando, Florida, college programs began recruiting me. One day, a Duke assistant by the name of Chuck Daly (later of NBA coaching fame) came to Orlando during the summer between my junior and senior years to watch me work out. I was ecstatic. I played as hard as I knew how. Duke was watching me!

Over the next several months, they wrote me letters from time to time. I was hoping for a scholarship offer. Eventually, they stopped attempting to recruit me. They signed another player who played my position. Duke was no longer an option for me.

But North Carolina didn't stop showing interest in me. Coach Smith visited several times, as did the assistant coach, John Lotz. They eventually offered me a scholarship. I enthusiastically accepted.

Something dramatic happened when I committed to that scholarship. At that moment, my rabid loyalties to Duke University basketball ceased. Stopped. Dead. Forever. My new love for and loyalties to North Carolina began. I was a new creation. The old had passed away. Duke was now the enemy. The new had come. I loved North Carolina. I've been passionately loyal ever since. I was converted. I was playing on the other team.

That's what happens with the Great Exchange. We exchange our old life for a new one. We accept a trade from one team to another. The old team, our old self, is now the enemy. Our old coach, the evil one, no longer dictates orders to us.

We have left the team of the kingdom of darkness. We have joined the team of the kingdom of light.

This begins our new loyalty to our new coach and team. Gone is our sin persona. We now hate sin, the old life, and all its decadence because we love something more: Jesus. New is our righteousness in Christ. He is our life's priority.

John Wesley, the founder of the Methodist tradition, said it well: "Give me one hundred people who hate nothing but sin and love nothing but Jesus and him crucified and I will change the world." Basically, he was saying, "Give me one hundred people who understand the Great Exchange and are totally committed to God's team, and I'll change the world. "

The Great Exchange and Daily Living

But I think there's more to understanding the power of the Great Exchange. It not only has to do with our eternal reality, though this is what's most important. It also has to do with now living day to day in God's strength and power as we play on his team. It should also affect our daily choices.

How? This is crucial, I think. We must understand how the Great Exchange informs our sense of identity.

Understanding the Great Exchange means we are able to rightly answer the question, "Who am I?" This is an essential question for all to be able to answer. In fact, the pastoral care department at the church I pastor, Forest Hill, has told me that if every Christian could definitively answer this question, knowing their new identity in Christ through the Great Exchange, 90 percent of Forest Hill's counseling workload would dissolve immediately.

Being able to answer this question in our culture comes with challenges. Why? Our culture is driven by mass marketing. It's everywhere around us. Consumerism and materialism are twin monsters daily trying to define our identity.

Groups of very smart people in New York City are spending countless hours and millions of dollars trying to figure out how to get us to spend our money on certain products. How is this done? They tell us that we are of no value unless we purchase product xyz. Our worth is found in what we buy, what we own, and how we look. It's not enough that we take some inches off our midsection. We need to have the six-pack abs of the guy on television (which will probably never happen to me no matter how hard I try).

Moreover, the marketers try to convince us that when we purchase certain products, we will then become a part of the "brand." Our worth and identity are defined by the same people who purchase the same product we purchase. We enter a community of people who share a similar brand, who then tell us that we are okay because we've purchased the same products they have purchased.

Marketers know the primary needs of consumers. One of, if not the most important need, is identity. They are trying to persuade us to buy a certain product that will make us feel like we are a person of worth and that we belong to something greater than ourselves.

When it comes to the Great Exchange, this one-sided *trade*, we are not only forgiven, but we now have a new identity. Before the trade, we were lost sinners, aimlessly being wooed by the temptation and the desires of the flesh. We were missing the mark of what God intended in our lives.

But now we are forgiven. We are "partakers of the divine nature" (2 Peter 1:4). We are holy, different. We are adopted sons and daughters of the King of kings and Lord of lords (Romans 8:15). Royal blood pulsates through our veins. We are heirs of everything our eternal Father owns in heaven. This adoption is final, never to be taken away. We are new creatures in Christ—the old has passed away and the new has come.

Put another way, our relationship with Jesus now defines us. We are not defined by the rejection of a person, or the loss of a job, or wearing a certain brand, or a disappointment that we don't look like a supermodel. We are not defined by what we feel in the moment, or our life experiences.

No! No matter what, we know our eternal Father loves us. Our identity is totally wrapped up in him. The Great Exchange now defines us. We believe what Jesus says about us, and not the lies and outside voices speaking to our souls.

Refusing to Listen to the Voices

Let's talk for a moment about those outside voices just mentioned. In Psalm 42:5, we find David doing something rather interesting: He's talking to himself. He's speaking to his soul. Based on his words we can determine this must have been during a time of disappointment, sickness, sorrow, pain, or discouragement. He asks, "Why are you cast down, O my soul...? Hope in God."

David was speaking words of life to his soul. He was saying, "Choose faith over fear. Choose hope over anxiety. Put your trust in the one who created you!"

Could it be that David understood that someone is speaking to our souls all day long? That there are "outside voices" constantly verbalizing lies to us? Psychologists call it self-talk. But I don't think the voices are from us. I believe these voices are from the hidden demonic world. The lips behind these voices hate God and those who serve him. They can use people, or media outlets, or radio waves to speak to us. Or they can invade our minds from seemingly nowhere.

When these voices speak, there is one major weapon they utilize to paralyze the follower of Jesus: condemnation. These voices constantly assault the truth of the Great Exchange and our new identity in Christ. They forever attack the promise that we are a new creation in Christ and our righteousness in him is secure. They incessantly assault the eternal message that God loves us unconditionally.

Conviction Versus Condemnation

Please note here the important difference between condemnation and conviction. Conviction is a work of the Holy Spirit. Because of the Great Exchange, he lives in us. When we sin, we grieve him. Because he loves us, he will convict us of our sin so we can repent. When conviction occurs (and it does within every follower of Jesus), we need to eliminate the behavior that hurts the Father's heart. Because he loves us, he wants it removed. It's keeping us from becoming all he wants us to be. It's preventing us from being close to him.

Conviction is a good gift from a loving Father in heaven. It disciplines and corrects us so our relationship with the Father can't be hampered.

Conversely, condemnation does not come from God. Romans 8:1 makes it very clear that "there is no condemnation for those who are in Christ Jesus." Condemnation comes from the evil one and his myriad minions. It does not convict us of sin, but of identity.

In other words, conviction addresses something we do. Condemnation condemns us with regard to who we are.

Conviction says I've done something bad. Condemnation says I am bad. Conviction says I've failed. Condemnation says I'm a failure.

Let me take this a step further. We are "righteous," accepted by God, based on one of two alternatives. We either possess a "righteousness according to the law," based on our works. Or we have a "righteousness according to Christ," based solely on Christ's work on the cross. If our righteousness is according to the law, whenever we break God's law, we should feel condemned. That's because our relationship with God is threatened. Therefore, we will hear the inner voice of condemnation.

But if our righteousness before God is based on Christ and Christ alone, on the Great Exchange, there is no law or work that defines our identity. We are in Christ by faith and faith alone. That's why Paul says in Romans 8:2: "For the law of the Spirit of life has set you free in Christ Jesus from the law of sin and death." We are free from the voices of condemnation because the law of sin and death no longer defines our identity before God.

If we feel condemned, it's because we've identified, in our minds, a law that we think is necessary for us to obey for God to love us. It's that simple. The Bible calls this "works righteousness." It means we are letting our identity be formed by what we do.

Again, when conviction occurs, all we need to do is repent of what we know is breaking our Father's heart. However, when condemnation occurs—when we are feeling as though we are worthless, useless, we'll never change—what should we do?

Like King David, we can speak to our soul. We can recognize the source of the voice we are hearing. We can say, "Don't buy that lie, soul. I'm not defined by what I do. The law doesn't define my identity. No! I've put my trust in God. I am the righteousness of God in Christ. I've accepted the Great Exchange. Even if I do sin, if I confess it, I'm forgiven, for God is faithful and just (1 John 1:9). Don't be downcast, my soul. You put your faith in God. I choose to believe that I am made righteous before God by grace through faith."

Conviction attacks behavior that the Father yearns to change. Condemnation attacks you and your identity in Christ. But there's no condemnation for those in Christ Jesus. Once the Great Exchange has happened, your identity can never be changed and is eternally secure. It's a free gift from God. Once traded, it can't be rescinded. The papers have been signed. The league office has approved the deal. The trade is forever final.

That's why it's called the good news.

A Lesson from My Granddaughter

Here's an illustration from my family. My wife, Marilynn, and I have been blessed with a beautiful granddaughter named Anna Grace. We have enjoyed watching her learn to crawl, then stand on wobbly knees, and finally walk. It made us relive memories of our own three children going through these stages.

I was watching my son-in-law Ryan and my daughter Bethany coach and coax Anna Grace to walk. They were extraordinarily patient. Whenever she fell, they laughed and encouraged her to get up and try again.

Now, can you imagine them berating Anna Grace for falling? Can you imagine them saying, "You stupid kid! Why can't you learn to walk? You're dumb for continuing to fail and fall. You'll always be a failure. You're worthless."

Of course not! No loving parent would say this to a child. Like Ryan and Bethany, you'd encourage your child to get up and keep moving toward your loving, outstretched arms. This is your child. She is a part of your life. You love her. You want her to succeed. Yes, you'll discipline her and "convict" her of sin when necessary. You don't want her to behave in ways that would hurt her.

But you want your child to know that her identity as a member of your family is never questioned. Your love for her is not predicated on how she performs a certain "law." There is never condemnation for your children who came from your heart of love.

Christians do fall and fail. But here's what the Great Exchange means: When you fall, you can get back up again and move toward the loving Father, not away from him.

When a person is under condemnation and falls, he is fearful of God's punishment and runs away and hides from God. He is afraid of being punished for wrongdoing. He feels like a failure.

This is not the position of a Christian who knows the truth of the Great Exchange. When followers of Jesus remember this truth, they get back up and keep running toward the Father. They understand grace. They know his love and acceptance. They remind their souls about the Great Exchange, which says that their identity does not rest in their performance.

Condemnation is a major weapon the evil one uses frequently to attack our identity and the Great Exchange. To be forewarned is to be prepared. Constant condemnation and how you respond to it will reveal whether you truly understand the reality of this Great Exchange made possible by Christ.

Conviction and condemnation are speaking to your soul every day. Which voice are you listening to? Which one "gets your ear"?

The next illustration will help you discern which voice gets the ear of your soul.

A Final Illustration

There's an old story about a frog getting ready to cross a swollen stream. A scorpion tapped him on the back and asked for a ride across the stream. The frog responded, "Of course not!" The scorpion asked, "Why not?" The frog responded, "Because you are a scorpion and we are mortal enemies. If you jump on my back and I give you this ride, you will sting me." "No I won't," the scorpion protested. "I promise I won't do this. Besides, we both need to get to the other side."

The frog waited a few moments, pondering the problem. Finally, he gave in and the scorpion jumped on his back. About halfway across the stream, the frog suddenly felt a stinger plunge into the back of his neck. The poison slowly seeped into his system. He knew that he was going to die. He turned toward the scorpion and asked, "Why? Why did you sting me?" To which the scorpion responded, "Because I'm a scorpion. That's what scorpions do."

If you believe you are a scorpion, you will behave like a scorpion. That's the message of this parable. Belief defines behavior. Your identity determines your actions.

But if you believe you are a child of God and you've made the

Great Exchange, you will be a different person. Your life can never be the same. You have traded your sin-stained soul for God's perfect righteousness and forgiveness. You have traded your obsessions for his perfection. You have traded your sorrows for his joy. You have traded your shame for his eternal approval.

It's a trade everyone should make.

I believe it's the greatest trade in the history of humankind.

When made, it makes you great in the sight of God.

And you've moved from superficiality to significance.

QUESTIONS TO PONDER

The Great Exchange is where the Christian faith begins. It's foundational for walking faithfully with God during our days on earth. We all need to make sure we fully understand its meaning and significance in our lives.

Here are some questions I regularly ask myself to make sure I totally understand and appreciate the Great Exchange in my life. I hope they help you as well.

1. Do you truly understand that Jesus died on the cross on your behalf and that the cross Jesus died on should have been your cross? Describe what Jesus did for you.

2. Do you believe that God poured out his wrath on his Son instead of you? What does this mean to you?

3. Do you ever contemplate that you deserve hell and eternal separation from the God against whom you've often rebelled? Describe how this makes you feel.

4. Have you made the Great Exchange? If so, describe how it changed your life.

5. When you ponder the meaning of the cross, does your arrogant and selfish human pride become offended? Why does this happen?

6. After you've received Christ as Lord and Savior, do you really believe that God sees you as perfectly righteous? Describe how God now sees you.

7. Is there any inconsistency between your identity in Christ and your behavior? If so, how?

8. When you hear voices of condemnation, what do you do? When you hear God's voice of conviction, what do you do?

9. When you fail, do you run toward or away from the Father?

10. Do you believe it's possible for anything that you do to ever separate you from the Father's love?

11. How much has the culture defined your identity? Be very honest.

12. Is your master passion in life to please the one who died for you? Give examples of how this is shown in your life.

CHAPTER 2

A GREAT FAITH

Coach Dean Smith won 879 collegiate basketball games. He is in college basketball's Hall of Fame. Generally, he is considered one of the greatest coaches in all of sports, not just basketball.

One feat for which he was noted was how many games he would miraculously win in the final seconds. They were games where most everyone believed the outcome had already been decided. But Coach Smith found a way to win.

One of his most famous victories of this ilk occurred in 1974. UNC was down by eight points with 17 seconds to play against its rival, Duke University. Bobby Jones, an All-American on that team, recounted to me those final 17 seconds.

In a series of bizarre events, UNC stole a pass and scored. Coach Smith called a time-out. UNC then fouled a Duke player. He missed the free throw. Coach Smith called another time-out. UNC advanced the ball and scored another basket. There was another missed free throw and another time-out. Finally, with just a couple seconds left, Walter Davis hit a shot at the buzzer. The game went into overtime and UNC won it. It was an incredible, amazing, miraculous victory. It's a game still talked about in college basketball circles.

As astounding as this victory was, there was something else that stood out even more to Bobby. He said, "Each time in the huddle, during the time-outs, Coach Smith would describe what was going to happen next. And it happened, every time, just as he described it. It got to the point that if he had said to me, 'Bobby, go into the far corner, get on all fours and bark like a dog and we'll win,' I'd have done exactly what he said!"

Why would Bobby have obeyed Coach Smith like this? It's because he had great faith that what Coach said would come true.

Great faith is absolutely essential for an inferior to have with a superior.

Developing Great Faith

Like Bobby Jones and several hundred other players, I had the privilege of playing under Coach Dean Smith. I remember him telling teams I played on over and over again, "The key to your success is you must believe in me. I've studied under some of the game's greatest coaches. I have had years of coaching experience. I've studied game films relentlessly. I've watched you play many times. Trust me. I know what I'm saying."

We had to believe he knew what he was doing and that he was in control throughout the game. We had to believe his philosophy of coaching worked.

I've never forgotten that. Great faith in him was the key to success. Just like a great faith in God is key to experiencing his miraculous power, being great in his eyes, and moving from superficiality to significance.

Giving instructions to one of his "players," the apostle Paul said to Timothy, "Fight the good fight of faith" (1 Timothy 6:12). It's good to fight the fight of faith, to strive in life to have a great faith. At the end of his own life, looking back over his life's "game," Paul said, "I have fought the good fight, I have finished the race, I have kept the faith" (2 Timothy 4:7). To have achieved a great faith is a good goal in life.

Would God Say You Have Great Faith?

Like an athlete fighting against a foe for victory and ultimately winning because he believes in the coach, similarly, to be great in God's sight means to fight the fight of faith and to develop a great faith.

Here are a couple questions for you: If you could hear Jesus say that one thing in your life was "great," what would you want that to be? Would it be that you have a great faith?

In Matthew 15, a Canaanite woman came to Jesus with a dire need. Her daughter was possessed by a demon. At first, Jesus remained silent. Then the disciples tried to keep her away. Finally, Jesus said to her that the Father had sent him first to the Jews, not to Canaanite Gentiles. There was every reason for her to give up. But she didn't. She knelt beside him and begged, "Lord, help me" (verse 25).

Jesus responded, "It is not right to take the children's bread and throw it to the dogs" (verse 26). Jesus used the term "dog," a common term used among Jews of that day toward Gentiles. It was the view of the disciples who were trying to send her away. But she wouldn't give up. With great wit, she responded, "Yes, Lord, yet even the dogs eat the crumbs that fall from their masters' table." Basically, she was saying, "I'll even take a crumb of your grace if that means my daughter will be well. Please, just give me a crumb."

Then comes verse 28. Jesus said, "O woman, great is your faith! Be it done for you as you desire." And her daughter was healed instantly.

Jesus said her faith was great. Can you imagine? Would the Lord of the universe ever compliment your faith as "great"?

Jesus said essentially the same thing to a Roman officer who came and asked for him to heal his servant. He believed it wasn't necessary for Jesus to go directly to his house to work this great miracle (Matthew 8:8). He believed Jesus could just speak a word or utter a prayer from a distance, and the miracle would occur. Jesus was overwhelmed by this man's faith. In fact, he said, "Truly, I tell you, with no one in Israel have I found such faith" (Matthew 8:10).

Jesus affirmed the Roman officer's great faith. Can there be a greater compliment?

Conversely, when Jesus visited Nazareth, his hometown, the Bible tells us he couldn't perform many miracles at all. I guess familiarity does breed contempt. A prophet is without honor in his own country. As

Mark concludes telling this story, he says that Jesus "marveled because of their unbelief" (Mark 6:6). Personally, I would never want the Creator of all to marvel at my unbelief toward him. I would want him to marvel at my great faith.

I am convinced God wants us to have great faith. He wants us to believe in the only biblical definition of faith: "Faith is the assurance of things hoped for, the conviction of things not seen" (Hebrews 11:1). He wants us to see that he rewards great faith to those who "diligently seek him" (Hebrews 11:6). He wants us to walk by faith, not sight (2 Corinthians 5:7). God wants great faith that produces mighty miracles, and that helps us realize the truth of God's words to us: "Not by might, nor by power but by my Spirit" (Zechariah 4:6).

Unquestionably, this kind of faith is not easy. It's a fight. It's a battle. It's a "fight of faith," as Paul called it (1 Timothy 6:12). There's an enemy. He wants to kill great faith. Why? Because he knows the key to victory in life is faith. Make no mistake about it: When Jesus comes back, that which he desires most to find in the hearts of his people is great faith (see Luke 18:8).

Do you have "great faith"? Would Jesus say that your faith is great like the Canaanite woman's faith? Would he commend your faith and marvel at it, as he did the Roman centurion's faith? Or would he marvel at your great "unbelief" as he did the Nazarenes' unbelief in his own hometown?

I don't know if God would call my faith "great." I hope so. I know that's my heart's greatest desire. My wonderful wife Marilynn tells me the greatest gift I've given to the people I've served the last thirty-plus years at Forest Hill Church is my great faith. I hope she is correct.

But here's what I do know: I have learned some valuable lessons in my faith walk over the course of three plus decades of life, marriage, parenting, and ministry. My hope is those lessons can help you grow your faith from "good to great," to use leadership guru Jim Collins' term in his book of the same title.

At Times, There's a Fog of Faith

John Kasay is a good friend of mine. For 15 years he was the Carolina

Panthers' placekicker. Though he finished the final year in his career as a New Orleans Saint, he is not only the Panthers' all-time leading scorer, but he is also in the top 10 in NFL history.

He's also a totally devoted follower of Jesus (and that's what I and many others, especially his wife, Laura, and his kids, love most about him!). He has positively influenced tens of thousands with his kicking and his faith. In my opinion, he has "great faith."

I'll never forget one particular field goal John lined up to kick. It was in the closing seconds of a key game. The kick would win the game for the Panthers. John did all his usual disciplined preparations for the kick. He visualized in his mind all the fundamentals that had always worked for him in kicking. He gauged where he was on the field. Finally, he threw a few blades of grass into the air to determine wind direction. The wind was blowing a bit in one direction, but not very hard. He knew what he had to do.

The ball was snapped. The holder placed the ball on the ground. John took a step toward the ball. Then something mysteriously unexplainable happened. Right at the moment of striking the ball, a gust of wind came from nowhere. It was totally unexpected. As the ball rocketed off John's foot, the wind blew, sending the ball on a path that went just outside the right goalpost. John missed the field goal.

Game over. The Panthers lost.

After the game, reporters encircled John to receive an explanation. One of the things I've always admired about John is he's a stand-up guy. He doesn't offer excuses. He tells it like he sees it. He said, "A gust of wind suddenly came and blew the ball wide right." Everyone saw it. It was undeniable. What no one could do was explain it.

Sometimes, in the fight of faith, winds come from nowhere and blow your ball off course. There's no practical explanation. It just happens. You do your best planning. You live as well as you know how. Yet still the wind blows out of nowhere. In this fallen, broken world, sometimes things just don't work out like you've planned.

Life's "sudden bursts of wind" can come out of nowhere and change your life forever. Because of the possibility of the unexplainable and the unexpected, you live in a fog of faith.

What do you do when mysterious winds blow your ball outside the goalposts? How does someone continue to have a "great faith," a faith Jesus would marvel at, when the unexplainable and unexpected happens to us? For it most certainly will happen to us all in some form or another.

I've learned from my life experiences that you must continue to believe. You must press forward in faith. You must trust the God who controls the wind when footballs are kicked outside the goalposts and painful experiences occur.

The apostle James wrote, "Count it all joy…when you meet trials of various kinds" (1:2). No one is immune to bad winds, rains, and storms in life. No one is immune to life's trials and tribulations, pains and persecutions, defeats and diseases.

When these trials come, I've found it helpful to recite from memory Deuteronomy 29:29: "The secret things belong to the LORD our God, but the things that are revealed belong to us and to our children forever." I recite it over and over again.

Sometimes God reveals what he is doing. But other times he doesn't. Those fall into the category of "the secret things" of the Lord, or "the fog of faith." That's why I'm convinced the most-often-spoken word in heaven is going to be "Oh" as God explains to us why he allowed life's winds suddenly and unexpectedly to blow our life's kicks off course. In heaven, as he answers our "Why?" questions, we'll constantly say, "Oh," "Oh," and "Oh." Today we look through a mirror dimly (1 Corinthians 13:12). Someday we will see face-to-face and understand.

Here's my question for you: When those secret mysteries occur, will you still believe? Would you still have great faith? Does your faith trust the sovereign God of the universe no matter what? Jesus knew difficulties would happen to us all. That's why, upon his return, he wants to find us still fighting the fight of faith. He wants us to trust him when bad things happen.

That's a very important aspect of having great faith. In fact, it's probably the testing ground to see how "great" our faith really is. I believe that when we continue to believe amidst these mysterious, unexpected winds, God especially "marvels" at our great faith.

Being Expectant and Great Faith

Many athletic contests have that one moment when the entire game changes. One team will be playing in a way that most certainly bodes for defeat.

Suddenly, a play occurs that changes the game from a loss to a win. Often, it's the great coach who makes a decision that turns the tide. Sometimes it's a gifted athlete who does something astounding through his God-given talent.

Similarly, the one in whom we have great faith, our great Coach, the Lord Jesus himself, can change the direction of our lives in an instant. I've experienced this personally (though it didn't happen in an athletic event). One such change took place in a fifteen second time period, yet forever changed my life and the lives of future generations.

As a young man, I always believed God had a special woman for me. Admittedly, I became nervous as I entered my midtwenties without having found her. I had dated a few girls, but nothing really clicked with any of them.

I did have one girlfriend in my midtwenties whom I had thought might be the one. But she rejected me (Can you imagine doing that to someone as wonderful as I am?). Looking back, I've come to believe even more in great faith that rejection is God's protection. She was not the one God desired for me to marry.

After that particular rejection, I released my concern to the Lord. I silently prayed, "Lord, I know rejection is your protection." Yet something within me kept saying, "Believe! Have faith. It's not over yet!" I began to believe there was someone. I learned that instead of being mad at the "ex" I needed to prepare for the "next." Instead of agonizingly waiting for the right person, I decided in faith to become the right person...and wait expectantly with great faith.

So I did...even though the months melted into years without this conviction and faith being realized and fulfilled. There was certainly a "fog of faith" at times as I waited.

After I entered seminary, I took leadership of a college age ministry at a church near the seminary I was attending. I made some close friends. The ministry also attracted some spiritual seekers who were not exactly walking deeply with the Lord.

One day, one of those "spiritual seekers" in the group came up to me and said he had a girl he wanted me to meet. He said our "auras" matched. (Mine was green and hers was gold, he informed me. *Wow, how weird*, I thought!) I'd played basketball with him several times, but I wasn't greatly impressed by his spiritual depth. So I casually and politely disregarded his request.

But he persisted. He gave me a sheet of paper with the name *Marilynn* on it. He said she went to Tucker High School and the University of Georgia. It had her phone number on it. That's all the information he had and he urged me repeatedly to call her.

I kept ignoring him. He kept persisting.

Frankly, I imagined this poor girl sitting by the phone, pining her heart away, and waiting for me to call her. A pang of sympathy vibrated through me. But I still didn't want to call her. By this time in life, I'd been set up one too many times. I did not want another bad, boring, and uneventful blind date!

Then I remembered something. A girl in the college group I oversaw, Donna, had gone to Tucker High School and would have been a year younger than this Marilynn. I called Donna and told her my predicament and gave her what little information I had on this Marilynn. Donna said the only person she knew who would fit this description was Marilynn Brame. Then she coyly said, "If it's her, are you ready to fall in love?"

Admittedly, my heart skipped a beat. Really? Fall in love? I still believed God had this plan for my life. Inwardly, I tenaciously clung to the promise. But it had been so many years! What should I do?

Okay, I'm a coward. I admit it. I was excitedly curious, but I didn't want another bad blind date. What to do? I asked Donna if she'd be willing to call this Marilynn and see if her last name was Brame. With a laugh and a good jibe against my cowardice, she agreed (now that's a real friend!). She called back within a few minutes and said, "Yep, that's her. Now call her and fall in love!"

I called her. We talked for almost two hours. We had so much in common. I asked her out that Saturday. She said yes. We went rafting. A several-hour date turned into an all-day affair. Three months later, we were engaged. Nine months after meeting her, we were married. (I know. I broke every premarital rule I give people. "Give it the test of time. Wait to be sure.") But we both just knew. Three decades-plus later, three kids and several grandkids later, we love each other more today than when we first met.

One other insight I need to give you on this story. When my basketball-playing friend met Marilynn, he was visiting her new roommate in Atlanta. Marilynn was more than four hours late arriving at her apartment that day because her car had broken down. When she met my friend, they passed each other on the stairs and simply said, "Hi." That's it. That was their total interaction that day. If Marilynn had been 15 seconds later, or if my friend had walked out of the apartment 15 seconds earlier, they'd never have met. The timing was perfect, God-ordained, and orchestrated under his perfect control.

Our entire lives, and the lives of our children and grandchildren and future generations, were forever and unalterably changed by 15 seconds of God's perfect plan for our lives.

For faith to work, we must expect God to move, even in a moment when we least expect him to move. We must believe he can change our life's game in 15 seconds. That's how great faith looks at life.

Yes, we need to trust God's providence in all, especially when life hurts and we're in the fog of faith. However, faith is also a gift from God that needs to be utilized. "Your faith has made you well," Jesus said repeatedly to people. Faith looks at circumstances and knows God is able to change them in an instant. We know he is able to do so, exceedingly and abundantly above all we could ever imagine (Ephesians 3:20).

We read the Scripture and see that people with "great faith" used God's sovereignty as the last stop on the journey, not the first. They knew that to begin prayer with a sigh and run immediately to God's providence and say, "Thy will be done" most often produces sloppy saints, indolent faith, and what someone once called "Prayerless prayers." They knew great faith must always be expectant and persistent to be powerful.

No matter what your situation, for faith to be great, you must believe that God can change your entire situation in one moment, with one decision, with one new circumstance. You are to live on the tiptoe of expectation for God to change your life.

The two words you should say most often in your great faith life on this side of eternity should be "But God." Your circumstances may be awful, "But God." Things may seem hopeless, "But God." Until God says the game is over, it's not over. Only God sounds the final buzzer.

For example, Marilynn battled infertility for eight years. Though doctors told her we would most likely never have children, she believed God had promised her a child. It fueled her faith. It was an expectant faith.

One day, I fell into despair. I asked Marilynn, "But what if we never have a child?" I'll never forget her answer. Sternly, she looked into my eyes and said, "David, if we're still childless and I'm on my deathbed, tubes running up my arms, seconds away from death, I want your ear to come to my lips to hear my last words. They will be a question to you: 'Am I pregnant yet?'"

Some of her friends used to tell her she lived in denial. They said that she needed to get in touch with her pain and grieve her loss. She refused. She said such thinking killed her expectant faith. She kept saying, "But God."

By the way, it's now three kids later. All three were conceived strangely, mysteriously, powerfully, sometimes Marilynn and I would say even miraculously. They were all conceived by God's grace through prayer and great faith.

Miracles and Great Faith

In my many years of life and ministry, I've seen miracles come through great faith. One of the most striking occurred in the 1970s. I was playing on a Christian basketball team touring Eastern Europe. We were using basketball as a means for spreading the gospel of Jesus Christ. We would play the game, and at halftime, a player on the team would share his testimony and the gospel with all who were present.

What made this experience unique though was the fact that we were traveling in countries behind what was then called the Iron Curtain. Many people were not friendly toward the gospel. They did allow us to give testimonies at halftime, but nothing more.

We always tried to go further, to push the envelope. We would try to hand out tracts and Bibles after the game to anyone with whom we had the opportunity. We knew it was strictly forbidden. But we were convinced God wanted us to do it. For us, our highest priority was to be faithful to God no matter what.

We played a game in then-Communist Yugoslavia against a team that had not lost on its home floor in years. Amazingly, we upset them. Because of our basketball prowess, people listened to the halftime testimony with greater intensity than normal. After the game, many surrounded us and wanted to talk.

Feeling courageous, we started to hand out tracts and Bibles to anyone interested. We had many takers. We left the city intoxicated with joy, excited beyond words, overwhelmed with gladness in the ways we knew God was using us.

We drove to our next destination. We arrived at the hotel only to find a message waiting for us from the organizer of our tour. He told us to leave the country immediately. There were orders to arrest us for distributing Christian material, primarily Bibles.

We left the country immediately and crossed over safely into Italy.

We were then confronted with another problem. We still had games to play in other Communist countries. We also had hundreds of Bibles we wanted to deliver to the underground church, especially in Poland, where persecution against Christians was great. It was strictly forbidden for people there to have Bibles.

What should we do? Should we risk being arrested in other countries? Several of the guys on the team had recently gotten married. Going to prison was not how they wanted to spend their honeymoons and start matrimonial bliss. Admittedly, those of us who were single weren't very excited about spending any time in a Communist prison either.

Conversely, we thought about all the Christians in those countries who had no Bibles. They lived by faith daily without a copy of God's

Word. Were we possibly God's instrument for bringing to them the truth in his Word? What should we do?

I'll never forget the team meeting we had in Italy to discuss our options. Everyone expressed the different options and their opinions. There was silence. We were torn between fear and faith. Finally, our coach, Linus Morris, stood up and said that we really had no option. Our brothers and sisters needed us to deliver God's Word to them. We were called to faithfulness. We had to believe in faith that God would protect us—indeed, deliver us if necessary.

We all prayed and sensed the same thing. We thought about how we could hide the Bibles in different storage compartments. Perhaps we could put them into boxes and pray that the checkpoint guards would not look into them. Yet none of our schemes gave us peace.

We concluded that the only option was to put the Bibles openly on the floor in the front seat of the vans. They would be in plain view. If asked by guards what they were, we would quizzically ask, "Bibles?" and go from there. We would plead ignorance if pushed. We chose great faith. Then we would trust God for our futures.

What happened next was nothing short of astounding. Over the next several weeks, we went through twelve different Communist checkpoints. Sometimes we stayed at a checkpoint for as long as four hours. Guards would search every van thoroughly. At one place, they made all of us open our suitcases and athletic bags. They rummaged through every inch of the suitcases and bags (though I bet our awfully smelly socks and other apparel shortened the search).

Here's the amazing miracle: Not once, not one time, did any checkpoint officer ever look in the front seat of the vans. Not once!

At times, this almost seemed comical. It was as if an angel himself was watching over us. Guards with serious expressions, submachine guns strapped to their shoulders, fervently searching our vans, yet never looking at the most obvious place where they would find something for which they were searching.

How our faith grew!

However, the most meaningful part of the trip was when we delivered the Bibles to the underground Christian church in Poland. The people who received them caressed them like they were holding precious diamonds. In their minds, they were. They wept. They profusely thanked us. I'll never forget it.

How did this happen? The only way I can explain it is a miracle of great faith. We believed God was able to protect us. It wasn't presumption. We just knew, deep inside, God was calling us to deliver the Bibles, and he would protect us.

He did.

God could never have blinded the eyes of those guards unless we had, by faith, obeyed him and moved toward those Communist checkpoints. Faith and obedience were inextricably connected. Together, they produced a great faith.

Final Thoughts

Remember: To have great faith is a battle and struggle. The enemy of your soul, the devil, does not want you to possess great faith. He will try every trick imaginable to rob you of great faith. When he fights against you, don't give in. Hold up the shield of great faith. Though his fiery darts will continue to come your way, your persistent faith will extinguish them. You are more than a conqueror through him who loves you (Romans 8:37).

The enemy of your soul especially despises it when he does his worst to you and you continue to possess great faith. When this happens to me, I can almost hear him swearing in frustration, snarling, "You mean I did all that to you and yet your faith is still great? How can that be?"

Great faith must persist and remain strong. It's not dependent on circumstances or feelings. It's rooted solely in God's promises. Jesus is the one who said great faith moves mountains (Mark 11:23).

Like we players at UNC believed Coach Smith's words to be trustworthy and true, which led to many miraculous victories, I believe God's Word. It says that God is great and nothing is impossible with him (Matthew 19:26). Because he is great and omnipotent, all can have great faith in him—the author and finisher of our faith (Hebrews 12:2). And we too can experience many miraculous victories in life.

Would God call your faith great?

Would Jesus marvel at your faith?
When your faith is great, Jesus marvels at it.
You are great in the sight of God.
And you've moved from superficiality to significance.

QUESTIONS TO PONDER

At this point, you may be wondering, "Well, how do I know if my faith is great or small?" Below are some questions for you to ponder to help you determine how great or small your faith may be.

1. Elijah was a man just like you, yet his fervent prayers moved God's hands. Are your prayers fervent (James 5:17)? Describe a time of fervent prayer in your life.

2. Do you ever have tears when you pray? Do you ever cry out to God? Have you ever prayed a desperate prayer like childless Rachel, "God, give me a child or just go ahead and take me home?" (see Genesis 30:1).

3. Are your prayers persistent? Do you mumble a request and then sigh in resignation, "Your will be done"? Or do you keep on asking, seeking, and knocking, as Jesus instructed me to do in Matthew 7:7? Give some examples.

4. Are you a worrier (which shows unbelief) or a warrior (which shows great faith) with your prayers? Give some examples.

5. Do you speak to your life's mountains about the greatness of your God, or to God about the greatness of your mountain? Give some examples.

6. Do you agree that two very important phrases for guarding great faith are "My God is able…" and "But God"? Are these two phrases ever a part of your prayer life and faith declarations? Do they fuel your faith? If so, how?

7. Do your words express great faith or are they words of complaining about your circumstances?

8. Do you ever say, "I just don't know," yet still possess great faith? If so, how?

9. Can you still praise God when you are in a fog of faith? If so, why?

10. Can you give God glory when things aren't working well for you? If so, why?

CHAPTER 3

THE GREAT REVERSAL

Every great golfer knows this truth: "It's not how you drive, it's how you arrive." What's most important is not how you drive the ball down the fairway. Rather, it's how you putt. It is how you finish the hole.

That is true in basketball as well. You could make a great move to get to the basket. But what good is it if you don't "finish" the move? You need to score the basket. This principle is true in all sports. What good is it to play well for most of the game and lose it in the last minute—especially in the final seconds of the game? Nothing is more frustrating.

I believe this is Jesus' message about our lives in eternity when he taught Matthew 19:27-30. Peter is saying to Jesus that he and the other disciples had left everything to follow him. Then he asks Jesus: "What then will we have given to us?" In other words, what will be our reward for giving up everything to follow you?

Jesus assures them that anyone who has given up something here on earth for his sake and the advancement of his kingdom will be rewarded in heaven. And it will be a great reward.

Then the zinger comes from Jesus in verse 30. It should cause all to pause: "But many who are first will be last, and the last first." I'll let your mind run wild for a moment as you try to think about what this may look like.

In my case, I immediately imagine a long line of people going into heaven. Those closest to Jesus are the saints on earth who, while on earth, have sacrificed everything for him, especially their lives. They labored tirelessly and anonymously for him. They suffered mistreatment, beatings, persecution, and even death for believing in Jesus in hostile environments. Because of their deep faith in him, friends and family rejected them. By contrast, Jesus warmly greets and receives them. He gives them great eternal rewards and blessings.

At the end of the line I find myself along with many other preachers and Christian leaders. We had influence and acclaim here on earth. People came in throngs to listen to our messages publicly, on radio, television, online, through our books, blogs, tweets, etc. Our salaries, while mostly not excessive, allowed us comforts most in the world don't come close to having.

What we might describe as persecution for being a Christian would be seen by those at the front of the line as a gnat swarming around their eyes, a mere annoyance. There would be no comparison between the two.

At the final judgment, Jesus is describing how people finish. Basically he is saying this: The last here on earth, those who seem to have little earthly influence but are faithful to the finish, will be first in heaven. And the first here on earth will be last in line there.

It's what some call the "Great Reversal." There will be no objections from anyone. All will find it fair in God's economy.

Repeated Constantly by Jesus

Three biblical teachings come to mind when I contemplate the Great Reversal.

First, there is Mark 10:45. James and John (and perhaps their mother, Salome, too) had approached Jesus about sitting on his left and right hands when he established his kingdom. We are told that when the other disciples heard this request, they became "indignant"— probably out of concern that their own desire for power was being squeezed out.

As the disciples jockeyed for power before Jesus' eyes, he told them that they were thinking like the power mongers in the world. That's not the way his disciples should think. Then comes Mark 10:45: "For the Son of Man did not come to be served but to serve and give his life as a ransom for many." Jesus' disciples are called to serve, not be served.

Second, Jesus echoed this teaching in Matthew 23:11, where he addressed the hypocrisy of the Pharisees. He pointed out their showy lifestyles. He spoke of their desire to sit at the seats of priority and privilege when people gather, to be celebrity superstars in their culture. He said, "The greatest among you shall be your servant." True greatness is defined by serving.

Third, I thought of John 13:1-13. We are told in Luke 22:24 that before the disciples met with Jesus in the Upper Room, they debated among themselves which one was the greatest. Jesus arose and took a towel and a basin of water and washed all their feet. In the Great Reversal, his disciples would wash others' feet as evidence of their desire to serve, not be served.

The first in God's kingdom are servants. The last are those who want everyone to serve them. The first are those who are humble. The last are those who want to be exalted.

Lessons from Burundi

Forest Hill Church, the church I've been privileged to oversee and lead for more than three decades, has developed a relationship with the general church in Burundi. When I mention the name of this country, few indicate they have even heard of it. It's about the size of the state of Maryland, and it's shaped almost exactly like a human heart. It's located in south/central Africa, wedged between Rwanda and the Democratic Republic of Congo.

Forest Hill Church became involved in this tiny country for three reasons. First, it is the victim of what some call the silent genocide. After the tragic genocide in Rwanda in the early 1990s, during which almost one million people were killed in three months, both Hutus and Tutsis spilled over into Burundi to escape the slaughter. Though they changed locales, their hatred for each other didn't change.

For the next 15 years, the genocide continued. Almost 800,000 people were killed. This received little to no press, unlike the enormous amount of international attention given to Rwanda's genocide. That's why it's been dubbed "the silent genocide."

The pain and scars of almost 20 years of genocide motivated Forest Hill to enter this environment as God's agent of peace and reconciliation. We have built a reconciliation center in Bujumbura, Burundi, the capital city—hopefully, prayerfully, to be a place where tribal/ethnic entities from all over Africa can come together under the banner of Jesus Christ and seek forgiveness with one another.

The on-the-ground partner is named ALARM—African Leadership and Reconciliation Ministries. We realize there can be little hope for future prosperity until the senseless cycle of revenge killing ceases. Through Jesus, these people learn that true forgiveness is giving up their right for revenge.

Second, we entered Burundi because it's the second-poorest nation on the face of the earth. There are many reasons for its poverty, not the least of which were the years of genocide. Along with this poverty was the problem of hunger, especially in the northern part of the country. Genocide, poverty, and hunger had enveloped a nation few knew or cared about. It was as if the souls of the departed had shouted into Forest Hill's leaders' ears, "Please come here! You must get involved."

Finally and most important, we entered Burundi because God called us to do so. It was an unmistakable call. We knew we had to go. We obeyed.

During our visit there, I was teaching a pastor's conference. I use the term "pastor's conference" with a smile. There were 45 pastors. We met in a hot, dusty, dimly lit conference center. I was invited to teach these pastors about preaching, something I love to do.

During the course of my teaching, I gave opportunities for several of them to share their stories. Most of them were pastors of small churches, most no larger than 50 or so members. In fact, most of them oversaw several churches at the same time!

They taught, oversaw, and cared for God's flock faithfully.

Almost everyone had the same story: they'd survived genocide and been tortured for their faith. Many had deep wounds, including brand marks and scars all over their bodies, because of their unashamed faith in Jesus Christ. Yet there was no bitterness. They sang and worshiped with a joy I'd never ever seen before. Their harmonious singing sounded like that of the angels in heaven singing.

Here I was, my large, white, 6'8" non-scarred basketball frame, with more blessings than I can describe, trying to teach preaching to guys whose faithfulness embarrassed mine. Who will be first in heaven?

And then there's Prosper. Yes, that's his name—Prosper, my interpreter in Burundi. He is a young man of uncanny intelligence and will. He is kind, sensitive, and a totally devoted follower of Jesus. He stood faithfully by my side and interpreted my messages to the pastors.

Sometimes he'd laugh at me when I got careless and used an English idiom he didn't understand. But he did a great job of making my words come alive to the listeners. In all the times I've taught in different cultures, he's absolutely the best interpreter I've ever had.

I'll never forget sharing with these pastors about Moses being denied entrance into the Promised Land. He had been disobedient to God, and this was his punishment. Then I shared the story of Jesus' Transfiguration. I shared how Jesus took Peter, James, and John with him on the mount. There, on the mount, Elijah and Moses appeared to Jesus and the three disciples.

I said, "Isn't it amazing how great God's grace is? Yes, initially, God didn't permit Moses to enter the Promised Land with the people. But he *did* allow Moses eventual entrance into the Promised Land. Moses' feet *did* eventually touch the soil there. And that happened in the presence of Jesus, his Lord and Savior, the Creator of the universe. God is the God of grace, mercy, and kindness. He redeems the worst of our situations and makes them new!"

To me, this was simply an interesting biblical observation. I wasn't ready for what happened next. Spontaneously, the pastors stood up and started wildly applauding God. They whistled, stomped their feet, and yelled continuously and joyously. It went on and on for almost a minute! They wouldn't stop praising and giving thanks to God.

At that moment I realized that they understood the true character of God, who makes all things new. As God did with Moses, they knew a God who takes pain and gives new life. They knew how God redeems brokenness, even genocide, for his glory.

That's how Prosper explained this phenomenon to me. These men knew God's profoundly amazing grace.

On my last night during that visit in Burundi, I asked Prosper to come by my room at the hotel. Some men in Charlotte had given me several hundred dollars to be distributed to whatever need I saw in Burundi. They knew the nation's extreme poverty and hunger. They wanted to help in some small way. I decided to give Prosper a part of this money for all his faithful labor to me.

Prosper sat on the bed. I told him about the men in Charlotte who had asked me to give a gift to people in Burundi. I gave him $200. At first, he was stunned. Moments of silence filled the air. Then he started to weep uncontrollably. When he finally got hold of himself, he told me how he arose every morning at 4 a.m. to pray. He specifically chose that hour because he wanted to beat the Muslims to prayer. (If you don't know, the Muslims begin every morning with prayer at 5 a.m. over an intercom that usually can be heard throughout the city.)

Over the past few weeks, he had been praying for God's provision in his own personal life. He made very little money. Making ends meet every day was a burden for him and his family. He truly prayed, "Give us this day our daily bread," and meant it. And he believed God would always provide. "And he always does," he said to Marilynn and me as he gently caressed the American dollars just given to him.

By this time, I had tears in my own eyes. I realized how blessed I am. I heard the Lord's voice within say, "Be generous, David."

I then reached into my wallet and pulled out every bill I had and gave it all to Prosper. I turned to Marilynn and said, "Please do the same." She followed suit, tears in her eyes as well! We had credit cards. We could use them to get back to the States. Prosper needed our money more than we did. $200? In America, people would spend that for a family dinner at a relatively nice restaurant.

Prosper had labored faithfully and tirelessly for the kingdom of God amidst abject poverty for years in Burundi. He loved Jesus more than anything.

Then it hit me: My overflow is his basic need.

Here's my point: In heaven, those Burundian pastors, and I think especially Prosper, are going to be at the front of the line, near Jesus. I'll be at the end. I asked Prosper, "Should we both die before we meet again in heaven, would you be so kind as to come to the end of the line, retrieve me, and introduce me to my eternal Lord and Savior?"

It's another example of the Great Reversal. In heaven, everything that is important there is not considered as important here. The first will be last. The last will be first.

How to Fight the Battle

To be great in God's sight, live out the Great Reversal now. How do we remain servants and resist celebrity superstardom at all costs?

It must begin with a full-fledged and relentless onslaught on pride. We begin with the conviction that God is God and we are not. It's the refusal to read our press clippings. It's the refusal to believe we are great. It's descending to greatness. It's the absolute belief that everything we have, everything we own, is a gift from God. Our physical strength and mental acumen are all loaned to us from heaven. We are to live for his glory and his glory alone.

Another way to fight this battle is to diligently pursue humility. Now, humility is not thinking *less* of us. Rather, it's minimizing thinking of self at all.

More Biblical Insights

Several verses from the Bible come to my mind when I think about humility. The first is James 4:10: "Humble yourselves before the Lord, and he will exalt you." Note the first two words: "Humble yourselves."

Then there is Matthew 11:23. Jesus said that the greatest among you is a servant. He follows this verse with these words: "Whoever exalts himself will be humbled, and whoever humbles himself will be exalted" (verse 24).

When you put these verses together, they give us powerful instructions about humility.

First, humility is not optional. Rather, it's an imperative. Followers of Jesus are commanded to be humble. How does this happen? The answer is found in the next point.

Second, it's a choice. We are not forced to be humble. We can choose not to obey God. But the verse in James implies that if we don't choose humility, God will not exalt us. We won't experience his eventual, eternal blessings in the Great Reversal.

Moreover, James 4:10 and Matthew 11:23-24 imply that if we don't choose humility, God will choose humility for us. I'd rather choose humility today than have God choose to teach me humility at some future date. Who knows how he may choose to do that? It could be an unpleasant experience, like a father disciplining a son (Hebrews 12:4-13). So it's important to learn this life lesson now.

Another verse that speaks powerfully about humility is found in James 4:8. It says, "God opposes the proud, but gives grace to the humble." Think about God opposing the proud. Think more specifically about the meaning of the word "opposes."

One of the fiercest rivalries in collegiate sports is one between the UNC and Duke basketball teams. One of my Duke friends once said to me: "I can't root for UNC in anything. I'd cheer against UNC if they played against ISIS." While he said that in jest, it serves as an example of someone who adamantly "opposes" another.

Now imagine God opposing us with that same kind of energy. He does so with one specific kind of person: the proud. He wants to defeat the proud the same way Duke wants to defeat UNC and vice versa. Pride is an opponent not to be coddled, but obliterated.

My wife Marilynn understands this truth better than anyone I know. In high school and college, she was very successful. In the eyes of the world, she had a grand future. A pathway to worldly success was in her grasp. But she knew something was lacking.

What changed her? It was chapter 8 of C.S. Lewis' *Mere Christianity*. That chapter is about pride. In it, Lewis tells how the devil became the devil because of pride. It is basically competitive. It's never satisfied with having enough. It must always have more. It's never content with being the best someone can be. It must always be better than someone else.

This was what nailed Marilynn. She knew she was driven by inexhaustible pride. She knew she had to be the best in everything she desired. She was convicted of her condition. She grieved over her sin. She repented of her pride. She became poor in spirit. She mourned. And God comforted her with his grace.

To this day, when she smells pride in me, she confronts it. She knows how deadly it is. It's arsenic to the soul.

Can pride be overcome? Yes, but the only antidote to pride is humility.

E.M. Bounds wrote:

> To be humble is to have a low estimate of oneself. It is to be modest, lowly, with a disposition to seek obscurity. Humility retires itself from the public gaze. It does not seek publicity or hunt for high places, neither does it care for prominence. Humility is retiring in its nature. Self-abasement belongs to humility. It is given to self-depreciation. It never exalts itself in the eyes of others or even in the eyes of itself...It has the disposition to praise others. "In honour preferring one another" (Rom. 12:10). It is not given to self-exaltation. Humility does not love the uppermost seats or aspire to the high places. It is willing to take the lowliest seat and prefers those places where it will be unnoticed.[1]

Probably the most profound teaching Jesus gave on this subject is the story of the Pharisee and the publican (Luke 18:9-14). Jesus made it clear that there was no place for pride in his kingdom. The Pharisee was wrapped up in self-conceit. He shouted his virtues to God, despising the poor publican standing far off. He exalted himself. He was permeated with pride. He lifted himself up as being spiritually superior to the self-abased publican before him.

By contrast, the publican saw no good in himself. He was overwhelmed with his depravity and sin. He couldn't even lift his eyes to heaven. With a downcast countenance, he mourned, "God be merciful to me a sinner."

With great precision, Jesus drove his point home. The Pharisee went home unjustified, condemned, and totally rejected by God. The publican went home justified, forgiven, and totally accepted by God. Jesus concluded, "Every one that exalts himself will be humbled, but the one who humbles himself will be exalted" (Luke 18:14).

Humility excuses others' flaws, esteems the virtues of others, and easily pardons injuries. And it fears pride as the deadly, infectious disease it is.

God loves it when we choose total surrender to him with humility. He loves it when we give up our pride, our self-sufficiency. He loves it when we say, "Nothing in my hands I bring, simply to your cross I cling." He loves it when he has unrestricted access to our hearts…and we finally yield all to him.

Humility is the pathway to being first in heaven's line. It's a choice God wants all his followers to make.

A Special Moment

There is a special and personal moment that has greatly informed my understanding of this call to humility.

It comes from Billy Graham. He was born in Charlotte, North Carolina. The farm on which he was raised is about a mile from the church I pastor. Charlotte proudly claims Billy Graham as one of her own—a native son. We even have a street named for him: the Billy Graham Parkway.

It was a no-brainer for the Billy Graham Evangelistic Association to move their headquarters from Minneapolis, Minnesota, to Charlotte some years ago. They purchased land right off the Billy Graham Parkway. They constructed buildings and offices. They even moved the original Graham homesite to this location. A library housing Dr. Graham's memorabilia is on the campus.

When construction was to begin on the library, several local pastors were invited to be a part of the groundbreaking. I was among them. I was greatly honored.

We gathered under a tent. It was excruciatingly hot. Yet there was an air of intense anticipation. Everyone gathered wanted to hear from the then almost ninety-year-old evangelist.

Dr. Graham entered and was seated on the platform. The service commenced. Dr. Graham was introduced to the hundreds of people gathered. He approached the podium. Immediately, everyone stood and loudly applauded. It went on and on. No one wanted to stop. It was easy to see that Dr. Graham was becoming increasingly uncomfortable and embarrassed by the prolonged, loud applause.

What happened next I'll never forget. Dr. Graham extended his hands, palms down, and beckoned over and over again for the crowd to stop clapping and sit down. It was a stark moment in contrasts. Hundreds of people were wildly applauding Dr. Graham while this aged, veteran saint was pleading wordlessly with his slightly trembling hands for everyone to stop and sit down.

Finally we did stop. We sat down. A reverent silence followed. Everyone was on the edge of their seats to hear his first words. He cleared his throat and said, "He must increase. I must decrease." He quoted the words of John the Baptist in John 3:30 as he examined his own life in relation to Jesus. It's one of my life verses as well. It's a desire of my heart. "He must increase, but I must decrease."

When Dr. Graham did this, I realized that he was opposing pride and choosing humility. He was being great in God's sight. It was a poignant, powerful moment in my life, one I'll never forget.

John the Baptist understood the key to following Jesus: humility. He knew, as his life advanced, that he must decrease and Jesus must increase. Billy Graham knew this as well.

More Biblical Examples

All the mighty people of God whose stories appear in the Bible knew the same truth.

For example, how beautiful is the lowly attitude of Abraham, God's friend, when he was pleading with God not to exhibit his wrath against Sodom. He said, "Behold, I have undertaken to speak to the Lord, I who am but dust and ashes" (Genesis 18:27). By the way, that's you and me too. I am continually amazed that God allows mere dust and ashes to come into his presence and worship him.

King Solomon appeared before God with a humble heart as well.

His wisdom was incomparable. His wealth was eye-popping and dropped jaws. Yet as he prayed before God, he said, "And now, O LORD my God, you have made your servant king in place of David my father, although I am but a little child. I do not know how to go out or come in" (1 Kings 3:7). This humility is why God felt he could entrust so much wisdom and wealth to Solomon.

The great apostle Paul considered himself to be "least of all the apostles" (Ephesians 3:8) and the greatest of all sinners (1 Timothy 1:15). That's humility! Perhaps that's why the Spirit entrusted him with writing two-thirds of the books in the New Testament.

Do you want to be "great" in God's sight? It's not found in the world's applause and success. It's not found in the world's power that desires to be served by others.

No, it's found in opposing pride and choosing humility, an acknowledgment that God is the Creator, the giver of everything. It's a desire to serve others above your own needs being met. It's choosing to worship the great God who alone is great.

The Great Reversal is about opposing the poison of pride, self-exaltation, self-aggrandizement, and self-congratulation. Those who are first in heaven will be the ones who chose humility.

A Lesson from My Dad

When I entered the ministry, my dad took me aside. He said he wanted to teach me the most important lesson he had ever learned as a pastor. He wanted to point me to the example of a biblical figure. I eagerly awaited his teaching.

What biblical character did he want me to emulate? Baruch. Have you ever heard of him? Unfortunately, not many sermons have been preached about him. He was a scribe who helped Jeremiah. Some would suggest he could have been the prophet Jeremiah's pupil and disciple—perhaps even his possible successor.

Dad reminded me of Jeremiah's words to Baruch in Jeremiah 45:5: "Do you seek great things for yourself? Seek them *not*." Dad then told me that ministry is not the place to seek great things for myself. I was not to use God's call on my life for my glory. I am not to use Jesus' bride, his church, for my glory. "Only God is worthy of all glory," he kept saying to me.

Sometimes I've heeded Dad's wise counsel. Sometimes I've forgotten it, much to my dismay. I know deep in my heart I want to decrease so that Jesus may increase. That is my heart's greatest desire.

Is it yours?

Final Thoughts

This chapter is my meager attempt to remind us that humility does not seek great things for personal benefit. True humility seeks only the applause of God. True humility seeks his glory alone. True humility knows we must decrease and Jesus must increase.

Humility is the essential quality of the Great Reversal. Those who are first here will be last in heaven. But those who are last here—the ones who operate in and choose humility to serve others on this side of eternity—will be first there. The first will be humbled. The last will be exalted.

Therefore, start choosing humility. Begin today, now. Live as a servant so that Jesus will increase.

It's essential to be considered great in the eyes of God.

It's absolutely essential when you want to move from superficiality to significance.

QUESTIONS TO PONDER

God doesn't force us to be humble. Humility is a choice. I have some questions I regularly ask myself so that I am reminded to stay humble. I call these questions my "humility tests." Perhaps you will find them helpful too for choosing humility.

1. How do you respond when someone corrects you, even if that person is your spouse or a close brother or sister in Christ who has your best interests at heart? Do you become defensive? If so, why?

2. How often do you simply take time to pause and reflect on the greatness of God? Describe these moments.

3. What's the first thought in your mind when your feet hit the floor in the morning? Do you see each day as a gift from God?

4. Do you ever pause to contemplate the reality of your next breath as a gift from God and how it could be lost in a moment?

5. How often throughout the day do you take time to thank God for all you have?

6. When you are complimented, is your first thought, "To God alone belongs all the glory"? Or do you say, "I worked hard for all I have!"?

7. Do you really believe the line in that great hymn, "Nothing in my hands I bring, simply to thy cross I cling"? Explain what it means to you.

8. What's your last thought of the day as your head hits the pillow? Is it "Oh, God, thank you for allowing me to live another day in this world you created"?

9. When you read Jeremiah 17:9, "The heart is deceitful and wicked above all else," do you consider that this could apply to your prideful heart? If so, how?

10. Do you praise God for the giftedness of others? When others' children succeed, do you celebrate their success?

11. Are you envious when others' children succeed? How do you handle their success when your own children don't succeed as much?

12. Do you ever fast? Fasting is a spiritual discipline we can turn to when faced with circumstances that are too big for us to handle. It's a way of expressing our total dependence upon God. It's a way of choosing humility.

CHAPTER 4

THE GREAT PARADOX

When I played college basketball in the late '60s and early '70s, no one lifted weights. It was considered counterproductive. If you bulked up, the theory went, you'd lose flexibility. Your shot would go away. Football players lifted weights. Basketball players didn't.

Going into my senior year in college, a machine was invented. It was called the Universal Weight Machine. A friend of mine in Orlando, Florida, where my parents were living at the time, had purchased one. He'd done hours of research on weight training and was sure it could help basketball players.

It didn't take long for my friend to convince me that a regimented training program on the machine would make me stronger without losing my shot. He said that I simply needed to go shoot baskets for at least thirty minutes after using the machine and my shot would remain the same. It seemed like a win/win to me.

That's exactly what happened. Faithfully, I used the machine each week. As a result, I did get stronger. My shot also stayed the same. And I had a profitable senior year.

The science of weight training is easy to understand. In lifting heavy objects, the muscle is broken down and becomes weak. Then the muscle is given a period of rest. During this time of rest, a powerful process inside the body begins. The muscle is built back up and becomes stronger than ever. And the heavier the weights, the stronger the person eventually becomes.

In weight training, when we are made weak, we're made strong.

It's a paradox. No, the definition of the word *paradox* is not two doctors (a terrible joke, I know). A paradox is something that seemingly contradicts itself but in reality doesn't.

Jesus gives us a "great paradox" about what it means to follow him: It's only when we're weak that we are made strong. It's only when we reach the end of our efforts that he can take over and make us strong.

From Jesus

Think about the following truths from Jesus:

1. Matthew 5:2: "Blessed are the poor in spirit for they shall receive the kingdom of God." Do you see what Jesus is saying? This is his first Beatitude. It speaks of the beginning point for life with him. Blessed people—those who receive the full blessing of God's kingdom—are poor in spirit. They are the broken of the world. They have no strength of their own. Life has depleted them of their own resources. Yet it's only in their paucity of spirit that God's kingdom can come alive for them. It's as if Jesus is saying: *"Blessed are the broken. Blessed are you when I tear down your strength. In your rest, I will build you up to be stronger than ever before."*

2. Matthew 5:3: "Blessed are those who mourn, for they shall be comforted." This second beatitude naturally follows the first one. After your life has been broken, you start to weep over your sin, depravity, and selfishness. You ache over the people you've hurt in your life. You know your life has not been what God intended. Yet when you cry over your brokenness, Jesus says that you are comforted. How will you be comforted? By the Holy Spirit. God's own presence will come to you and abide in you. He will assure

you of your forgiveness. He will walk with you forever. He will never leave you or forsake you. But God's powerful presence cannot come to you until after you are weak and weeping. There is no other way.

3. John 12:24: "Truly, truly I say to you, unless a grain of wheat falls into the earth and dies, it remains alone; but if it dies, it bears much fruit." This is the same truth we've already been looking at, but expressed in a different context. Unless we fall into the earth and die, we will not be able to bear much fruit for God. But when we let our outer shells of success, fame, fortune, self-exaltation, and narcissism die, and our greatest desire becomes glorifying God, we end up bearing much fruit for him. When our outer shells are cracked, only then can *his* life be released from within to serve a dying world.

Seems almost counterintuitive, doesn't it? But every bit of it is true. We become broken and the kingdom of God is ours. We cry and weep over our sin, and God gives us himself, his presence, strength, power, and comfort. We die to ourselves, and we bear much fruit for God's glory.

The Power of Prayer and Worship

It is through prayer and worship that we can express our brokenness and dependence on God. They give evidence to times when we realize that God is God and we're not. They declare God alone is worthy of all praise and honor. They say, "God, my life is totally in your hands. Without you, I can do nothing."

Think about the postures the Bible adjures all lovers of God to assume in worship and in prayer:

• We are to bow our knees. This is a position of powerlessness before a strong, sovereign Ruler.

• We are to lower our heads. This is a posture of weakness before someone more powerful than we are. We are not worthy to look into his eyes. The more powerful the person before us, the more he can do anything he wants to us. The lower our heads become, the more vulnerable we are before him. We've chosen to be weak and vulnerable in the eternal King's presence.

- We are to raise our hands. Several of the psalms exhort worshippers to raise their hands before the Lord. Paul says in 1 Timothy 2:8 that he wishes all men everywhere would lift their hands to God in prayer. What does this mean? No matter what part of the world you live in, this is the universal sign of surrender. No matter where you may be, if someone approaches you from behind with a gun and points it at your back, you immediately raise your hands. You are clearly saying to him, "I surrender." That's the meaning of your hands being raised in worship. It's saying to God, "I surrender all to you."

God likes people with bent knees, lowered heads, and raised hands. Why? It's because these positions express weakness. When we become weak, he becomes strong. When we relinquish control, he takes control. It's the great paradox.

It sounds almost un-American, doesn't it? Isn't there a cultural mantra that suggests that only the strong survive? Isn't life about the survival of the fittest?

That's not the biblical perspective. The Bible teaches that when we totally depend on God, we see him at work. When we completely trust him, he makes us strong. Two people can't steer a car together at breakneck speed. One has to yield to the other for the car not to careen off the road.

Lessons from Paul

The apostle Paul knew this truth. He was smart. He had risen to great power in the Jewish hierarchy in Jerusalem—a feat achieved only by people with extraordinary mental acumen. He was also a major persecutor of the early church, and he carried out his role with great zeal.

Then the resurrected Jesus appeared to Paul. He was chosen

specifically to be one of Jesus' apostles. God used his great mind. Eventually he wrote about half of the books in the New Testament. He must also have had amazing physical stamina, as evidenced by his long missionary journeys. If anyone could boast in his own strength, Paul could.

Yet in a debate with the false teachers in Corinth about his apostolic authority, he recounted his experiences that had made him weak. In 2 Corinthians 11, starting with verse 24, he mentioned:

- Five different times the Jews gave him 39 lashes (called "intermediate death" by the Romans because few survived even one of these beatings).
- Three different times he was beaten with rods.
- Once he was stoned.
- Three times he was shipwrecked.
- He spent a whole night and a day adrift at sea.
- He traveled many miles, with each mile making him increasingly weary.
- He faced dangers from flooded rivers, robbers, and from Jews and Gentiles, all of whom wanted him dead.
- He faced danger in the cities, in the deserts, and on the stormy seas.
- He faced danger and rejection from men who claimed to be Christians but in reality were not followers of Jesus.
- He lived with chronic pain and sleepless nights.
- Often he went hungry and thirsty for extended periods of time.
- Often he shivered with cold, without enough clothing to keep him warm.
- Along with these trials, he was burdened with how the churches he planted were getting along with one another and how vulnerable they were to false teachers.

Paul concluded this section of 2 Corinthians with these words in verse 30: "If I must boast, I would rather boast about the things that show how weak I am. God, the Father of our Lord Jesus, who is to be praised forever, knows I tell the truth."

He boasted in his weakness.

Continuing into chapter 12, Paul described a supernatural experience. He was lifted into heaven, caught up into paradise. He heard things spoken that were so astounding and marvelous they could not be told. Might he have heard information about how the world was going to be transformed? No one knows.

Paul did say that if anyone had a reason to boast, it was he, especially after this supernatural experience. From verse 5 onward, Paul said, in essence: "That experience is something worth boasting about, but I am not going to do it. I am going to boast only about my weakness. I have plenty to boast about and would be no fool in doing it, because I would be telling the truth. But I won't do it. I don't want anyone to think more highly of me than what they can actually see in my life and my message, even though I have received wonderful revelations from God."

Then Paul went on to describe his famous "thorn in the flesh," a "messenger from Satan" given to him "to torment me and keep me from getting proud."

What was this thorn? No one knows. Was it an illness? Some have speculated that it was malaria, contracted during his first missionary journey in the mountains of Galatia. Some suggest that he suffered constantly from migraines associated with malaria. Others say he experienced chronic pain from the beatings he received. Others say perhaps it was a broken relationship, perhaps even a divorce. A person had to be married to be on the Sanhedrin. Paul was on the Sanhedrin, yet he was single. Could there have been a divorce? If so, some speculate that his wife may still have been alive, and perhaps there were children. And when Paul thought about them, his heart ached in pain over his marital failure and fatherless children.

No one knows for sure what the thorn was. My best guess is it was people—more particularly the false teachers. In fact, the only other time we hear the phrase "thorn in the flesh" in the Bible has to do with the Canaanites being a "thorn in the flesh" of the Israelites (Judges 2:3). The only other time the term is used biblically is in reference to people.

Personally, I've had painful athletic injuries. I've had life disappointments. But the most painful experience I've had is people who work behind the scenes to undermine the ministry with which God has entrusted me. I'm talking about people who have been disloyal, even plotting and scheming subterfuge. I'm sure Jesus must have felt this pain when Judas betrayed him. I wonder if some of these false teachers may have even, at one point, been Paul's friends. When he lived in Jerusalem, had they served together on the Sanhedrin? The pain of friendship gone awry is one of the most painful experiences possible, in my opinion.

Again, no one really knows what the thorn was. However, Paul did give us one interesting fact about it: He said it was a messenger from Satan. It was not from God. How could it have been? God is not the author of evil. It is a result of the fall. Biblically, that's clear. Yet God permits evil. Not only does he permit it, he says that he uses it in the lives of his people for good and for his purposes.

Paul is an example of this truth. Three different times, he begged God to take this messenger from Satan away. God was certainly able to do so. Satan is just a creature; God is the Creator. He has authority over everything, including the demonic world.

Yet each time Paul asked God to take away the thorn, God said to Paul, "My gracious favor is all you need. My power works best in your weakness."

God purposely left the thorn in Paul's life to teach him that when he is weak, God is strong. He didn't remove it in order to teach Paul that God's power is perfected in weakness. He did not want Paul to become conceited—especially as he was privy to do since he had seen such marvelous visions in the third heaven.

There it is again: the Great Paradox. God's power works best when we're weak. Paul knew it. That's why he concluded this section of Corinthians with these words: "So now I am glad to boast about my weaknesses, so that the power of Christ may work through me. Since I know it is all for Christ's good, I am quite content with my weaknesses and with insults, hardships, persecutions, and calamities. *For when I am weak, then he is strong"* (2 Corinthians 12:10).

Oftentimes, our deepest need in the midst of chronic weakness is not quick relief but confidence that God is working through our weakness for a good purpose in our lives. God will not allow the thorn to be taken away because he knows self-sufficiency is on the surface, ready to rise again. Our total dependence on him is more important than the relief from the pain. Our complete reliance on Jesus is God's goal.

Yet when we have finally given up and yielded to God's power, the complete work of love is accomplished in us. In Jesus' weakness on the cross, the power of his resurrection life is released in us and into the world.

A Personal Lesson

I learned this lesson the hard way. I always wanted to be a strong leader. I'd thought that strong spiritual leadership meant seeing a hill, blowing the trumpet, and leading the charge. No prisoners would be taken. The victory flag would be planted on the hill no matter what. Everyone was expected to follow my lead.

In the early 1990s, I was convinced God wanted Forest Hill Church to go in a new direction. I had received a new vision. I called all the leaders together for a weekend retreat. I cast the new vision, ready to lead the way. The fellow leaders nodded their heads in agreement. I charged ahead.

The new plan was rather radical, especially compared to where we had been. I was trying to move Forest Hill to become a more outreach-focused church. The new vision was most evidenced in a change in worship, a movement to a more contemporary form that connected better to spiritual seekers.

Several months into the transition, I could sense discomfort, especially in the area of worship. People in the church were disquieted, even complaining a bit. This was unusual for me, for the church had long been healthy and complaints were seldom heard.

As is often the case, the complaints were spoken to others and not to me. In part, this was because the congregation loved me. They didn't want to hurt my feelings. But it was also because of this simple maxim: Leaders are often the last to know. Because of their position, they are often insulated from the results of their decisions.

Finally, the leaders called a meeting. They vigorously debated the new direction. I was surprised to hear certain people raising objections. Previously, they'd been stalwart defenders of my various dreams and strategies through the years. Not now. Not only were they not my defenders, they were outright critics.

Others wanted to give the new direction more time to see if things might naturally shake out for the good. Still others were excitedly following my plans. It didn't take me long to realize that we'd entered into crisis mode. It was a consummate logjam. We were stuck and divided. No one knew what to do.

In God's sovereignty, this logjam occurred right before my annual vacation. The leaders asked me to go away, pray, and seek God to see if this new vision was really where the Lord wanted us to go. I was ready for the break. All the tension had exhausted me. So I enthusiastically embraced the opportunity for time away. I knew I needed to seek God for help in finding a solution.

Just before I left, someone in the church gave me a little book by Henri Nouwen entitled *In the Name of Jesus*. The subtitle suggested the book was written to offer a new paradigm for leadership in the twenty-first century. I placed it among some other books, not knowing if I'd have the time or energy to read it.

One day during the vacation, a voice within kept whispering to me: *"Read that book."* At first I ignored it, but the voice persisted. I had learned to listen to and obey that voice. It was the Lord. Finally, I picked up the book and started reading it.

It was life-transforming. It's not a long book, nor was it difficult to read. Yet I laboriously pored over each page, sometimes reading one page several times. It was literary manna from heaven, spiritual food for a starved soul.

Nouwen suggested that in the twenty-first century, a new paradigm of leadership was needed to replace the old one (remember, I was reading this book in the early 1990s). The antiquated model, he offered, was a command-and-control kind, one in which the leader would see a hill and charge it, taking no prisoners, as he accomplished his goal. He expected all others to follow him.

Can you hear the "Ouch" that emitted from my soul as I read the book? It was as if Nouwen had been reading my own biography over the last several months.

The new paradigm, Nouwen suggested, would be a model built around servant leadership. The leader would be a servant to others, not using them for his own purposes, but serving them for their good.

Nouwen cited a biblical example of this from John 21. In a resurrection appearance, Jesus asked Peter three times if he loved him. Each time, Peter responded yes. Jesus was making sure that with each one of Peter's three denials spoken the night before he died, Peter would now hear three affirmations of his love for Peter. It was a way of restoring Peter's soul.

Then Jesus told Peter to "feed my sheep." He was placing Peter in the position of a pastor. Jesus knew that many would need to know what Peter had learned about grace and forgiveness. He wanted Peter to share with others how God's power is perfected in weakness.

Properly restored, Jesus then told Peter a day will soon come when people would take him to a place where he did not want to go. He was alluding to the day when Peter would be crucified for his faith.

What was Peter's response? He asked, "What about John?"

Isn't that just like us? We want to know if someone else will have as difficult time as we do. Jesus said to Peter: "Leave John to me. I'll do with John what I want to do with John. But you need to follow me."

Peter accepted the inevitability of what Jesus wanted from his life.

Nouwen concluded the narrative by saying that servant leadership in the twenty-first century will involve leaders who will be called to go places where they may not want to go. Authoritarian leadership will not be viable in the future. Servant leaders will have to collaborate with others and serve them if they want to be effective, even if that means going to a place where they don't want to go.

I read that section over and over again. It became clear to me what I had to do. I was willing to obey the Lord's will, even if it meant I didn't get what I had wanted.

The first night after my return from vacation was the regularly scheduled leadership meeting. I could tell that there was a mixture of electricity and uncertainty in the air. The church's future was being discussed. Inwardly, I knew my own future hung in the balance. The church leaders had the right to ask for my resignation if they desired to do so.

After the opening prayer, one of the leaders paused and asked me, "Well, David, you've been away for a couple of weeks. Do you have a leading from the Lord regarding our conundrum here? To where are we supposed to go?"

I told the group how thankful I was for the time away. I told them about the book I'd read. Surprisingly, I then said to them, "I think I'm supposed to tell you that I'll go to wherever you want to go. If you want to become a traditional church, I'll lead you there. If you want to be a contemporary church, I'll lead you there. If you want to become a blended church, I'll lead you there. My job is to serve you, not use you for my own satisfaction."

A deafening silence came upon the room. No one had expected this response from me. Several had expected a fight. Some had thought there'd be a rancorous debate. Others didn't know what would happen. But no one had expected to hear what I had just said.

Finally, after several moments of silence, one of the leaders said, "Well, David, where do you think we should go?"

I wasn't expecting that question. I paused. Finally, I responded, "Well, I still think the Lord wants us to be an outreach-focused church. I think he wants us to be more intentionally concerned for the lost who don't know him and the poor who desperately need our strengths and resources."

I paused again. More silence ensued. It lasted for a couple of minutes. Finally, one of the most influential elders said, "Well, everyone, I suggest we follow our leader."

The vast majority nodded in agreement. We began to collaborate together exactly what that meant.

I'd love to tell you everything was perfect afterward. It was not. Some leaders eventually left the church. Some people did too. But we became a unified leadership team. We tweaked different aspects of the vision that needed change. We moved forward in unity.

Suddenly, almost miraculously, from this moment onward, Forest Hill Church was imbibed with a new power. The entire church became unified like never before. We started to give our lives away. Lost people began to be saved in greater numbers. The poor were being served more than ever.

Today, Forest Hill is known throughout the Charlotte/Mecklenburg region as a church that regularly experiences the presence and power of Christ. It's a grace-filled church where any person seeking spiritual truth is welcome. It's a church that unashamedly teaches God's Word and truth. It's a church that gives its life away. We have earned the right to be heard by people throughout the area because of Christ's life pulsating through the veins of his bride called Forest Hill.

God took me to a place where I didn't want to go: giving up the vision in order to die to self and serve others. I had become weak. I was vulnerable. Yet, in turn, he empowered my weakness with his power and made Forest Hill Church even stronger. His power was perfected in my weakness. His grace was sufficient for me.

It's a lesson I've never forgotten. I never will. It's spilled over to almost every area of my life since then. Because I know I'm weak, I'm willing to listen to and collaborate more with others. Because I know I'm weak, I pray more. Because I know I'm weak, I'm convinced I'm not always right. Because I know I'm weak, my worship is deeper and richer. Because I know I'm weak, God's power can work in me. And I've seen God's power make Forest Hill great in God's sight.

More Biblical Examples

When King Jehoshaphat was outnumbered and surrounded by the enemy, there was no hope. Yet God reminded Jehoshaphat that the battle belonged to him. The king was told, "Trust me in this position of impossibility and watch my deliverance." He trusted in weakness and God gave him a mighty victory.

In the Psalms, when David was in dire circumstances, he cried out to God, "Arise!" In this one-word faith declaration, David was essentially saying to God, "Fight this battle for me. It's too great for me to handle. I have no strength to do so. The battle belongs to you." Over and over again, God delivered David, mostly amidst times of great weakness.

God loves the simple prayer, "Help me! I have no strength. Arise, Lord! The battle belongs to you. In my weakness, you are made strong."

When Jesus fights the battle and delivers us, he alone receives all the glory because the victory is totally his. We then are released, in humility and in his strength, to minister to others with "thorns" like ours (2 Corinthians 1:4). Who can better give them God's strength than those to whom God's strength was given in a similar circumstance? In our weakness, he is made strong!

On one occasion, Jesus was asked about giving to Caesar. His opponents were trying to trap him. He asked for someone to give him a denarius. It was a common silver coin in that day.

Its present-day value would be around twenty-five cents. I am struck that Jesus had to ask for a denarius. Apparently he didn't have one. Was that by choice? Did he purposely not possess any money? If so, that means that the King of kings and Lord of lords didn't possess a simple quarter. Yet he controlled the movement of the stars, the ebb and flow of the tides, the rotation of the earth. How amazing!

Jesus chose to leave the comfort, beauty, splendor, and power of heaven to come to this broken earth. He humbled himself in the form of humanity, taking on flesh to die on a gnarled tree to set us free from the power of sin and death.

Yet because of this act of dependence and weakness, God the Father lifted him up to a place of power. The resurrected Jesus, the King who had no quarter, now sits at the right hand of the Father in heaven, the supreme position of power and glory. From this place of honor, one day in the future, he will come to judge the living and the dead. And on that day every knee will bow, and every tongue will confess that Jesus Christ is Lord over all (Philippians 2:5-11).

On that great day, I know what I'll say to Jesus: "Lord, I am nothing. I am mere dust and ashes. I deserve eternal death. But I believe you were raised from the dead by the power of the Holy Spirit. I am so very weak. But you are so very strong. Your strength is perfected in my weakness. I praise you today and forever."

When I'm weak, he is strong. It's not what our culture calls strength. But from God's perspective, it is true strength.

It's the Great Paradox.

We are great in God's eyes when we realize it.

And we've moved from superficiality to significance.

QUESTIONS TO PONDER

Here are some questions that I regularly ask myself so that I remain strong in my weakness. I hope they are helpful to you as well.

1. What do you need to release to God in faith to see his power working more in your life? (Clue: It's most often in the area of your greatest strength.)

2. What's your prayer life like? Do you ever assume the position of bent knee, bowed head, or raised hands in your prayer time? Explain how these postures express weakness.

3. When have you seen God's power perfected in your weakness?

4. When you worship God, do you see it as an opportunity for you to proclaim your weakness to him and your dependence upon his strength?

5. Do you regularly thank God for that broken place in your life?

6. Is God's grace sufficient for you? Why or why not?

7. Do you seek collaboration from others when major decisions need to be made? Or are you absolutely convinced that you are always right?

8. When was the last time you yielded to another's view and simply trusted God?

9. When was the last time you asked your spouse for advice with a problem you have faced and followed it?

10. Would your work associates/spouse call you a control freak and an authoritarian leader? Why or why not?

11. Have you ever prayed to God, "Arise! This battle I'm fighting is too big for me. You must fight it for me"? Similarly, have you ever prayed to God, "This battle

belongs to you, Lord"? What happened when you finally let go and gave your problem to God?

12. Do you know someone who shares the same kind of thorn you have? Have you shared with that person how God gave you strength in your weakness?

CHAPTER 5

THE GREAT COMMANDMENT, PART 1

'll never forget the day when I received my first letter from the University of North Carolina basketball department. It had blue letterhead and blue ink and was signed by Dean Smith, the head basketball coach. It said they'd heard about my high school accomplishments and they were interested in me as a student/athlete becoming a part of their basketball program. They asked me to fill out a form and return it to them as soon as possible.

I did so. Inwardly, I was excited. Would this great school, with an incredible basketball tradition, really be interested in me? Would Coach Smith, new on the scene but rapidly becoming respected as a head coach, actually offer me a scholarship? Could this be possible?

Several months thereafter, I received a phone call from Coach Dean Smith. He said he was flying through Orlando, Florida, and wondered if my family and I could meet him at the Orlando airport for dinner. He said they were interested in my becoming a part of their program.

Mom, Dad, and I had dinner with him at the airport. Everyone was impressed with him.

Then I started receiving phone calls from John Lotz, the assistant coach at North Carolina. John's father was a Baptist minister in New

York City. John himself was a committed Christian, often speaking at different Fellowship of Christian Athletes events. He too visited my family in Orlando after Coach Smith did. All I remember about that evening is after he left, my Mom turned to my dad and said, "I like him."

My dad said, "I do too." That made an impression.

The letters and phone calls continued. During a Christmas tournament, I looked up in the stands and saw Coach Smith, unannounced. I knew he was there to see me play. Though the coaches at UNC were in constant touch with me, they had not officially offered me a scholarship. I knew why. They needed to see me play. It made perfect sense. Now Coach Smith was present to see me play.

I played well. Soon thereafter came the phone call I'd waited for. Coach Smith offered me a scholarship to play collegiate basketball at the University of North Carolina. Eventually I signed a scholarship to play at UNC, with Coach Smith in my home. My parents were proudly watching. It was one of the more memorable moments in my life.

Interestingly, when I signed that scholarship, no one knew what Coach Smith would become. We didn't know he would later become a Hall of Fame coach. We didn't know he would win an Olympic gold medal and two national championships. We didn't know he would be selected the best coach in all sports by ESPN between 1975 and 2000. We didn't know that UNC would become a standard-bearer for college basketball excellence and success. We didn't know that "Carolina baby blue" would be a color worn throughout the world.

The reason UNC became very successful was because of Coach Dean Smith. Today, I am humbled and honored to think I had the privilege of playing for this great man in this great program. When people ask me where I played college basketball, I proudly say, "UNC-Chapel Hill."

In all honesty, sometimes I wonder, *Did I really play basketball at UNC? Did that happen?* I was a decent player, but I had my limitations. I didn't jump very high. I wasn't excessively quick. I wasn't greatly athletic. I just knew how to play the game. Yet Dean Smith offered *me* a scholarship to play for him.

Some days I compare myself to other UNC players and conclude I couldn't have been that good of a player. I think of players like Larry Miller, Charlie Scott, Phil Ford, Michael Jordan, James Worthy, Vince Carter, Ty Lawson, Tyler Hansbrough, Tyler Zeller, Marcus Paige, and others. I'm not even in their league.

But that's the very point I want to make. It really doesn't matter what I think of my own playing ability. My opinion doesn't matter. What matters is what Coach Dean Smith thought of me. When I wonder how good I really was, I remember that *he* made the first phone call. *He* made the first visit to my home. *He* first came to watch me play. *He* first offered me the scholarship. *He* initiated everything in our relationship. I chose him only in response to the fact and reality that he first chose me.

I stand in awe, every day of my life, that Dean Smith first wanted me. It doesn't matter what I think of my ability. The only thing that matters is what he thought of my ability. And he wanted me on his team. He first recruited me. He initiated the scholarship offer.

Learning to Love God

One day, Jesus was asked, "What is the greatest commandment of all?" He could have chosen any from among the 613 possibilities. He said, "You shall love the Lord your God with all your heart and with all your soul and with all your mind. This is the great and first commandment. And a second is like it: you shall love your neighbor as yourself" (Matthew 22:37-39). He encapsulated the entire Law and Prophets with this great commandment: Love God with all you have. And love your neighbor as you love yourself.

Jesus was saying that everything in your life should begin with the first part of what's commonly called The Great Commandment: You are to love God with all your mind, heart, soul, and might.

But before you can do this, you need to realize this great truth: God first loved you. First John 4:10: "This is love, not that we love God but that he first loved us and gave his life as an atoning sacrifice for our sin." Did you catch the primary point of this verse? Before you ever loved God, *he* first loved you.

Jesus said to his disciples in John 15:16: "You did not choose me, but I chose you and appointed you that you should go and bear fruit and that your fruit should abide, so that whatever you ask the Father in my name, he may give it to you."

Ephesians 1:4 states that God chose his children before the world was even created.

If you love God, you need to realize he first loved you. Before creation, God chose you and knew you by name. He loved you long before you ever loved him.

That means the almighty God of the universe initiated all contact with you. He wrote you the first letter to pursue you being on his team. He made the first phone call to you. He first visited you in your home. He was the one who asked you to play for him and be in relationship with him. He offered you the eternal, irrevocable scholarship to play for him on his team before you ever made the decision to accept it or not.

There are many days when I don't feel worthy in this Christian life. I look at my inadequacies, fears, and foibles and am perplexed that God would give me a second thought. There are many days when I compare myself to other Christians who seem much more faithful. I conclude that Jesus couldn't possibly want me on his team.

But he did. Though I'm nothing, mere dust and ashes, God desired me to be in his family, on his team. It doesn't matter what I think of myself. God sees me as worthy. He desperately wanted me on his team.

He chose me.

When I consider this reality, I fall to my knees in worship of this great God who first wanted me. I stand in awe of this great God who recruited me.

Yes, you are to love God with all that is within you. This is the greatest of all the commandments. Jesus said so.

You are never greater in God's sight than when you love him passionately. You are never more significant in God's eyes than when you worship him fervently.

However, you need constantly to pause and realize that the only reason you love and worship him is because he first loved you. He first recruited you. He first desired you to play on his team. He is the one who offered you the eternal scholarship.

The Meaning of a Covenant

This signing of the scholarship can be compared to a biblical covenant. It has nothing to do with emotions and circumstances. It is an irrevocable agreement, a commitment of the will. The closest human analogy to a biblical covenant is marriage.

The public vow expressed between a man and a woman is intended to be permanent. You say to your prospective spouse during the marriage vows, "And I do promise and covenant." A covenant cannot be broken. It is irrevocable.

Our life's conditions may be plenty or want, sickness or health, richer or poorer. It doesn't matter. You stay together. Why? It's because a covenant has been pledged. You are covenanted to stay together, in your wills, no matter what feelings you may have or how circumstances may change. You covenant to "forsake all others." Your eyes and heart are fixed forever on your beloved.

An Example from Dad

My dad clearly understood the meaning of covenant. I saw him honor his covenant with my mom. Her Alzheimer's disease devastated her mind and body over a period of 17 years. Yet I saw Dad faithfully remain by her side as her dementia perilously progressed. During those times when she was unable to recognize him, her gaze far away, days when he wondered if any cognizant memory existed in her mind, he sat by her, stroking her hand and telling her how much he loved her.

Once I asked him if he ever thought about leaving her. It was painful for me to watch him care for her. Surely God desired him to be happy. Surely God didn't want him to daily carry this burden on his back, incessantly sapping his strength for the rest of his life.

He lowered his head and responded, "No, son, I could never do it. I covenanted to my God and her that I'd stay with her forever. I made a covenant. This is sickness. This is want. This is poorer. But I'll never leave or forsake her."

Notice he used the word *covenant*. He clearly understood what the word meant. It meant loving forever.

Covenant in the Bible

Biblically, you see God's covenant in operation when he called Abraham out of the city of Ur. There it is again: God initiated the call to Abraham. There was nothing noteworthy in Abraham to make God commence the call. God simply did it. God would be his God. Abraham would obey with all his heart. And God would bless all the nations of the world through Abraham (Genesis 12:3). God blessed Abraham to be a blessing to the world.

Jesus made a new covenant with his people, the church (Luke 22:20). Every time a Christian partakes of the Lord's Table, it should be a reminder of the meaning of Jesus' new covenant. It is eternal. Just like my scholarship, it cannot be revoked. Communion reminds us that God will not take his covenant away from us. Every time the bread and wine are ingested, they serve as a reminder of his eternal love living inside his followers—a love he initiated in eternity.

God desired our lives to be filled with his love. It's an enormous gift, initiated and received by his great grace and mercy.

The Meaning of Grace and Mercy

Grace and *mercy* are two often-used Christian words. What do they mean? Why are they so important for the Christian faith?

These two words became alive for me one day when one of my sons directly disobeyed me. I was astounded. I had asked him to do something and he looked me in the eye and said, "I'm not going to do that."

I didn't often see this kind of defiance in him. I asked him again to obey me. He wouldn't budge.

My heart was filled with a mixture of anger and confusion. I told him to go to his room and wait for me. I said that I'd be upstairs in a few minutes to discipline him. He bowed his head, pouting as he shuffled his feet, slowing climbing the stairs to his room.

I gathered myself. I knew the teaching that you should never try to discipline your child when you're angry (though I'm not sure when a parent would then ever discipline his child). I thought through what I wanted to say and do. I wanted him to learn that he could not behave this way. His stiff-necked defiance needed to stop—for his own good.

After a few moments, I climbed the stairs as well and walked into his room. I knew what I needed to do.

But I wasn't ready for what happened next. I was expecting continued hard-heartedness. But that's not what greeted me at all.

Instead, my son looked up to me with tears in his eyes and began begging me not to discipline him. He did not want me to give him what he knew he deserved. He knew he had disobeyed and dishonored me. He knew he deserved his punishment. But he asked me for...*mercy.*

My heart was deeply moved by his contrition. I responded to his humble request with mercy. I did not give him what he deserved—the best definition of mercy I've ever heard. He deserved to be punished for his dogged disobedience. But his trembling body and contrite tears changed my mind. My heart was deeply moved. I chose to extend mercy to him.

I took him into my arms and held his still-quivering body. I dried his tears with my hands. I held him closely until he gathered himself.

I then asked him if he knew what he had done wrong. With tears still filling his eyes, he nodded yes. He said he didn't know why he did what he did. He said it was like something dark and foreign came over him.

I carefully explained to him the reason he needed to always and immediately obey me. I reminded him that I only wanted his best. I also said that when he disobeyed me, he was learning to disobey God—and I simply couldn't let that happen.

My son assured me he understood what I was trying to do. He asked me to forgive him. I gladly did. I kissed him on the cheek and reiterated how much I loved him and wanted the best for him.

I then carefully considered my next step. I knew I had a marvelous teaching opportunity staring me in the face. I knew I had a wonderful chance to teach him about the meaning of mercy and grace.

An idea hit me. I seized the moment.

I went into my bedroom and noticed a number of quarters on the top of my dresser. I quickly raked them into the palm of my hand and put them into the pocket of my pants.

My wife Marilynn was working in our bedroom. She casually asked me, "What are you doing?" She had heard this confrontation downstairs with our son from its inception, and was awaiting my discipline when I entered his room. She didn't know what had happened.

I told her what had just transpired. I then said to her, "I'm going to take him out for some ice cream." She smiled and said, "That's grace, David." I said, "You're right!"

It was grace. Not only did he receive mercy (not receiving what he deserved), he also got grace, receiving what he *didn't* deserve: ice cream.

Through the years, I've repeatedly used this story to help people understand the meaning of God's rich grace and mercy that Christians have received through Jesus (Ephesians 2:4). Many people have shared with me how this story has been like a light going on in their minds to help them understand these two very important biblical words.

Examine with me their true meaning.

When God in Jesus took the punishment for our sins upon himself, he didn't give us what we deserve (eternal condemnation and separation from him). What incredible mercy!

But God didn't stop there. He continually gives us what we don't deserve—ice cream: the next beat of our hearts, the air in our lungs, the food we eat, the clothes on our back, the privilege of living on his earth, our different friends and family members, experiencing the beauty of his creation, etc. *Plus* (and this is the most important aspect of his grace), he gave us the precious, invaluable gift of eternal life—an eternal relationship with his Son, Jesus—something we don't deserve. What amazing grace!

Why would God give grace and mercy to rebellious, stiff-necked, and disobedient children like you and me? Why would he ever want anyone to be forever members of his heavenly team?

The answer is simple: It's because he first loved you. He profoundly loves you. He chose you. Among all the people on the face of this earth, he wanted you on his team. He has an incredible plan and purpose for you. You're not an accident. You're not the result of random circumstances having been formed from primordial sludge. You were created by him and for him.

You can't really follow Christ faithfully unless you hear and understand this message from God: how much he loves you. And he loved you long before you ever loved him.

Where It Should First Be Heard

God knows how important it is for every person to hear this life-changing message. And I think he wanted us to first hear it from our earthly fathers. That was his original design. He wanted kids to hear and experience unconditional love from their earthly dads. Through their words and actions, kids would feel that nothing could ever separate them from their dad's love.

God knew that when this rightly happens in homes, it would become much easier for kids to hear and understand this message about his love when he began to reach out and start recruiting them to his team.

That was certainly my life experience. God gave me a dad who expressed unconditional love to me throughout my life. Yes, he loved me enough to discipline me when needed. It hurt, but I knew he was doing it for my own good.

Dad also extended grace and mercy to me when I needed it. There were several times he gave me what I didn't deserve, only to turn around and extend to me more than I could ever deserve.

Dad modeled for me what good fathering should look like. I tried to emulate his example with my three kids. What he gave to me, I tried to give to them. I hope I succeeded. That was my heart's desire.

Dad died several years ago. His ninety-year-old body finally exhausted itself. He died peacefully in his sleep as the clock by his bed struck noon. I'm certain he immediately went to the heavenly Father he loved and served most all his days on earth.

I miss him terribly. He was a good and godly dad. And I'm convinced that I love God today largely because of how much dad loved God. I emulated who he was. The God he personally knew through Jesus was the God I wanted to know. He was real to dad. Therefore, I wanted to know this reality.

Eventually, I came to personally know dad's God. He has become my close friend and companion. I've learned to love him with all my heart, soul, mind, and might. Dad helped me know that the only reason I love God is because he first loved me.

After Dad died, I was rummaging through some old books. In one of them, I found a birthday note Dad wrote to me on July 6, 2006. Here's what he wrote:

> Dear Son,
>
> This isn't the traditional birthday card, but I hope this sheet and its contents will convey to you the most profound feelings of my heart on this coming Sunday, July 9 [my birthday].
>
> If Mom were with us [she had passed away the year before] in person, I'm confident she would join me in assuring you that you have exceeded any expectations we may have held for the baby we welcomed to our home on July 9, 1949. Through your ministry, your family, and the wonderful way you have touched and impacted the lives of myriads we are inestimably grateful we can call you "our son." We pray someday you may say the same for your sons.
>
> With my undying love,
> Dad

I never tire of reading these words from my dad. Every time I do, they give life to my soul.

Every Child Needs to Hear These Words

As I grew up, I knew Dad was proud of me. It had nothing to do with my earthly performance. It was simply because I was his beloved son whom he loved.

Pause for a moment and think about this biblical reality. Not once, but twice, Jesus heard these words from his eternal Dad: "You are my beloved Son and I'm proud of you!"

The first time was at his baptism. Jesus spent 30 years waiting for his Father in heaven's perfect time to leave his earthly family to begin his messianic calling. We don't exactly know how this call came, but it did.

Jesus approached his cousin John and asked him to baptize him (Matthew 3:13-17). Be aware that Jesus didn't need to be baptized. He was sinless in every way. He was giving us sinful humans an example of our need to be baptized.

Jesus insisted John baptize him. John obeyed.

Immediately after Jesus' baptism, the Holy Spirit descended from heaven upon him. He heard a voice that said, "You are my beloved Son, with you I am well pleased" (Luke 3:22).

The Father in heaven must have known the importance of these words for Jesus to hear as he inaugurated his ministry. Surely the Father knew they would persistently echo in Jesus' ears as he steadfastly persevered toward the cross. Surely he knew these words would give strength to his Son to face people's withering criticism, hardened unbelief, and rancid rejection.

Surprisingly, the Father gave these same words to Jesus a second time. As the reality of the cross drew nearer, Jesus took Peter, James, and John up on a mountain. While there, Elijah and Moses appeared to them. Jesus' body and clothes were transfigured into a shimmering, eternal brightness. A voice from heaven spoke and said, "This is my beloved Son, with whom I am well pleased" (Matthew 17:5). Surely the Father knew that his Son would be encouraged by this reassurance again as he faced the agony of the cross.

Jesus was perfect and sinless, incarnated in human flesh by the will of his Father. Yet his Father deemed it necessary, not once but twice, to assure him of his great love and calling. If Jesus needed these words from his Father to face life's challenging situations, how much more do we?

Every dad needs to make sure that he says the same thing to his kids—not once or twice, but over and over again.

My dad did it with me. I believe it's important for all dads to do so.

Think About This

Before I was ever conceived, my parents decided that they first wanted me. They chose to have me. I had nothing to do with them first loving me. There was nothing meritorious in me to make them want me. They wanted me just because they wanted me. They couldn't even see me. They knew nothing about me. Yet they still chose to have me.

If you are adopted, you should feel an even greater wonder over the love of your parents. From among all the possible adoptees in the world, they chose to adopt, love, and cherish you. They sought you. They spent countless dollars, oftentimes sacrificially, to bring you home with them. Was there anything worthy in you to woo their affection? Of course not! How could that even be perceived? They were motivated solely by an inward desire of love for you. That's why you were chosen.

When moms and dads love one another, they desire to express that love by forming a new life they both could love. They want their love extended to others.

That's the nature of God's love. As the Father, Son, and Holy Spirit perfectly and intimately loved each other throughout eternity, humanity was created as an extension of that love. God created us to pour out his love in us. He desired us to enter the love relationship.

That is the primary reason God made you and me. Let that reality sink deeply into your hearts.

God first loved us.

The Importance of Worship

There can be only one natural response to the knowledge of the Father's great love for you: to love him with all your heart, soul, mind, and might. You worship him with all that is within you.

When you do this, you become a true worshipper of the God who first loved you. Jesus deeply desires that his followers become true worshippers. In fact, he told the Samaritan woman that in the future, people would not be limited to an earthly place to worship. For the Samaritans, that place was Mount Gerizim. For the Jews, it was the temple in Jerusalem (John 4).

But after his death and resurrection, the God of the universe would now indwell the hearts of all those who believe in Jesus. Every second of every minute of every day, you know the love of the Father. You regularly hear his voice saying, "You are my beloved child. I love you. I'm so proud of you."

People can worship God no matter where they are or what they may be doing. Worship can take place while washing the dishes or wrapping up a multimillion dollar deal. Worship can happen while changing a diaper or charging a credit card. Worship can occur while driving to work or waiting for a doctor's appointment.

In times of great distress and disappointment, the Father's love is never doubted or denied by the true worshipper. It's always there. It is always present. Every day is spent in the Father's presence. He constantly hears from his children, "I love you, Father. With my prayers and praise, I express love to you. I worship you with all that is in me."

Why can you worship a God like this? It's because you know with certainty that he first loved you.

How great is the Father's love for you that he would call you his child (1 John 3:1). If you ever doubt this love, let your mind focus on two realities. First, look at the cradle. Think about the God of the universe leaving the splendor of heaven to live in the squalor of this world. Why would the holy God of the universe enter the filth of this world? He did so to pursue a love relationship with you. It's because of his great love for you.

Second, consider the cross. Think about the agonizing pain Jesus experienced—both physically and spiritually. The physical pain was excruciating (*excruciating* comes from the two Latin words, *ex crucis,* which means "from the cross"). Yet Jesus experienced this physical pain because of his love for you.

The spiritual pain was even greater. Imagine Jesus' worst nightmare: being separated from his Father. Yet when our sin was placed upon him, the Father could no longer have fellowship with him. Jesus no longer had intimate fellowship with his Father. It was an agonizing moment for Jesus. It's why he cried out, "My God, my God, why have you forsaken me?" (Matthew 27:46). Yet there on the cross you see God's forgiveness and love poured out for you.

The cradle and the cross prove the Father's love. Believe it's true. It's what develops a heart of worship.

Final Thoughts

How much the heavenly Father loves you! He wants you to be in a covenant relationship with him. He first loved you. He began the relationship with you. He recruited you.

How then should you respond? By understanding the full meaning of the Great Commandment. By loving him in return—with all your heart, soul, mind, and might. By becoming a true worshipper—worshipping him with all that is within you.

God then becomes the master passion of your life. You seek him and his kingdom above all else. With all that is within you, you love and bless his holy name.

When you receive and reciprocate his love, you are great in his sight.

And you've moved from superficiality to significance.

QUESTIONS TO PONDER

Here are some questions for you to ponder to make sure you fully understand the first part of the Great Commandment:

1. Do you know how much God loves you? Describe the first time you began to know his love for you.

2. What evidence can you point to as proof of God's love for you?

3. Have you ever contemplated the fact that God chose you and knew you by name before the world was ever created? How does this make you feel?

4. Do you realize that God's "scholarship" offer to you is irrevocable?

5. Is there anything that can separate you from God's love?

6. Is there something in your life that you love more than God? What is it? Can you give it up?

7. Do you love to worship God? Do you find yourself worshipping God throughout your day?

8. Does the reality of God's love calm your fears? Describe how.

9. If God began the relationship with you, are you confident he'd never leave or forsake you? Describe how this confidence affects your soul.

> "For I am sure that neither death nor life, nor angels nor rulers, nor things present nor things to come, nor powers, nor height nor depth, nor anything else in all creation will be able to separate us from the love of God in Christ Jesus our Lord."
> —Romans 8:38-39

CHAPTER 6

THE GREAT COMMANDMENT, PART 2

Yes, you are great in God's sight when you love him with all your heart, soul, mind, and might. It's in response to the fact that he first loved you. But that's not all. There is a natural expression of your love for God on this earth. You're also great in his sight when you love that which God loves the most: your neighbors, his children created in his image, who live among us.

How are you to love your neighbors? Jesus specifically said that you are to love them as you do yourself.

Think about it. Though you live in a world fraught with low self-esteem, even the person who loathes himself actually loves himself. Even the person with the lowest possible self-worth places himself at the center of his universe. He feeds, clothes, exercises, and entertains himself—daily and regularly. He spends most of his money and time on himself. He thinks of number one first before anyone else.

The same is true for every person who lives on this planet. You really do love yourself. You do prioritize your life above others' needs. No one is exempt from this wretched self-aggrandizement.

Jesus challenges this self-absorption with the Great Commandment. He pointedly says that if you love God, you are to love your neighbor like you love yourself. If you love God, you are to spend time, effort, money, and energy on your neighbors like you do yourself.

Jesus expressly said that loving your neighbor is a primary, purposeful way you express love to your heavenly Father.

An Example from My Life

One time a close friend gave one of my kids a very special gift. I was overwhelmed by his boundless generosity. It was unexpected, but very appreciated. It went well beyond anything that I could have ever wanted him to have. I was profoundly grateful.

My friend and I were having lunch together one day after he'd given this gift. Still deeply moved by his overwhelming generosity, I asked him why he had done it. I wanted to know his heart's motivation.

My friend didn't pause. He immediately knew the answer. He said, "Well, you've helped me grow immeasurably in my faith. Because of your teaching, I have eternity in my heart. There's peace within like never before. I'm a new person. The old has passed away. My wife, friends, and associates all see it. I'm now living with purpose. I see God's plan for my life daily unfolding before me. It's undeniable what has happened in my life.

"I was therefore trying to figure out a way to thank you. All kinds of different options entered my mind. It finally came to me. I suddenly realized that the best way I could tell you how much I love and appreciate you is by loving what you love the most: your kids. That's what motivated me to give the gift."

I have contemplated his words over and over again. And I've concluded that he's very right. In fact, he couldn't be *more* right. The best way to show love to me is to love what I love the most: my wife and children. I am happiest when I know they are happy. I love the old parenting adage: You are only as happy as your unhappiest child. It's very true. Even after they are grown, it's true. If they are unhappy, you're unhappy. But if they are ecstatically happy, you are equally happy.

If you want to love me, love my kids.

The same is true with God. If you love God with all that is within you, the best way to show it is by loving that which he loves the most:

his children. These people are the crown of his creation. They have his divine image stamped on them.

People who live around you and throughout the world are your neighbors.

After Jesus taught that the Great Commandment is the greatest of all the other commandments, a man asked him, "Who is our neighbor?" (Luke 10:26-30). Jesus' answer is specific. He basically responded by saying, "Yes!"

In other words, Jesus was teaching, "The entire world is your neighbor. Whoever is in need—God's kids everywhere, both locally and globally—is your neighbor. He may live next door. She may live across the world. But Jesus made it very clear: The world is your neighborhood. And all his children are your neighbors.

On God's Heart from the Beginning

The idea of loving your neighbor was on God's heart when he first called Abraham. The covenant God made with Abraham in Genesis 12:3 was simply this: "I will bless you so that you can be a blessing to the world." Abraham was blessed so that he could be a blessing. God would greatly bless him so that he could bless others.

The term "so that" is very important in God's economy.

My wife Marilynn came up with a great slogan that Forest Hill Church has consistently used in our different expansion campaigns over the years. It is a simple slogan: "So That." Bracelets have been made with the two words "So That" on them. Forest Hill members have worn them on their wrists throughout each campaign. Some have even kept wearing them after the campaign to remind them of the meaning of these two very important words.

On every communication to the congregation about the campaign, the two words "So That" were plastered everywhere. The leadership wanted these two words to be engrained into the minds of the people.

Why was this important? What did the slogan mean?

Marilynn once said to me that every human life is either a "So What?" or a "So That!" If you reach the end of your life and have done nothing to bless others, nothing to show God's love to your neighbors,

God may sigh and ask about you, "So What?" So what that you have accumulated possessions? So what that you've received the plaudits of the people of this planet? So what that you've had a good time in life?

That's not God's purpose for you. God wants your life to be a "So That." You receive God's rich grace and mercy so that you can give it away. Love isn't love until it's given away...to your neighbors, God's children, his most prized possession.

These people are your literal neighbors. They are hurting people who live next door to you or in your neighborhood. They are people for whom you can care with a helping hand, a cooked meal, an encouraging word, a face-to-face prayer.

But I'd like to enlarge your thinking. Your neighbors also include a local group to whom God calls you to love as your neighbor as well.

The Local Poor as Your Neighbors

The materially poor live near you. They are the sick, deprived, and hurting in your neighborhoods, schools, and churches. In many major cities, the poor are concentrated in a few segregated neighborhoods, mostly in the inner-city areas.

However, as property prices have boomed, and more and more people desire the benefits of life in and near cities, gentrification has happened. Wealthy developers have purchased this property, recognizing how future growth will increase its value.

As a result, many of the poor have been dispersed. Some have relocated in vacant apartments and mixed housing units. Others have moved away from the center of the cities. In other words, the poor have moved next door. You no longer need to drive into the inner city to serve the poor. They are in your midst, in your neighborhoods, in your schools, learning next to your child.

The church I pastor, Forest Hill, is located in south Charlotte. One of its campuses is about a mile from the South Park Mall, one of the most upscale malls in all of North Carolina. As you drive south on Park Road from the South Park Mall toward the church, then go down perhaps another mile, something astounding happens. If you turn left, you will turn into some of Charlotte's wealthiest neighborhoods. If you turn right, you will run into apartment complexes housing some of Charlotte's poorest citizens, many of them displaced by gentrification. They are also the sojourners, aliens, and immigrants trying to find a new life—ones whom God has commanded his people to love (Leviticus 19:34).

The poor have moved next door. They have little funds for food, clothes, books, supplies, and hygiene needs. They live day to day in dire straits.

Recently I was asked to be a part of a 20-person Charlotte Task Force. It was formed in response to a Harvard study of the United States' 50 largest cities and their ability to enhance upward mobility. When the study was released, Charlotte's leaders were strikingly surprised and embarrassed to discover that Charlotte ranked last in providing opportunities for upward mobility.

Charlotte had been proud to be known as a shiny new Southern city. Over the previous 30 plus years, it had become one of the nation's fastest-growing cities. People were drawn to its temperate climate, its location, and easy access to both the mountains and beaches. Charlotte also enjoyed ostensible advantages for job advancement and upward financial mobility—mostly because of the large number of banks.

But the study didn't lie. It was profoundly pointed in its analysis. Charlotte was last in moving upward out of poverty.

The task force spent almost two years together. We heard multiple presentations from different people and groups about the poor. We discovered a few things about the poor you many not know:

1. Many poor parents have to decide between taking a pay raise or keeping their children in needed preschool programs. A large percentage of the assistance they receive would be taken away if they accepted the raise. Their desire to work hard and advance in life is offset by the financial boundaries that determine whether they can receive aid. Surprisingly, many take the raise and lose the preschool aid. Their sense of accomplishment and modeling a strong work ethic for the children is more important to them

than a subsidy. But it threatens their children's crucial brain development at an early age. What would you have chosen?

2. If a child can't read by grade three, he most likely will spend the rest of his life trying to catch up. Those kids who can't read by grade three start to make the decision *then* to drop out of school later. Volunteers who are willing to go to read with kids in schools between pre-kindergarten through third grades can forever change the trajectory of a child's life.

3. A mentor who will walk with a child and help him navigate life's choices can make an enormous difference. Even an hour a week in a relationship with a vulnerable child can change a child's life.

4. Very often the most vulnerable and financially challenged student can receive necessary aid to go to college. But they usually fall short by about $5,000. That amount, given to them, can often be the difference in whether or not they can gain a life-changing college experience and experience future upward mobility.

Many other insights were given about the plight of these children. Many options are available to caring people who want to get involved and help. It's not a hopeless situation. Something can be done. And in our specific case Charlotte didn't have to remain last on the list.

Bringing change demands people with a caring will—especially people who say they love God—stepping to the plate and doing something for those in need. It means being people who are willing to choose to love their neighbors as they love themselves.

This should be especially true for those who know how much God loves the poor. It is impossible for you to ignore their existence. You cannot deafen your ears to their cries for help.

They are your neighbors, figuratively and literally. They are our kids as well.

The Global Poor as Your Neighbor

There is another neighborhood you may be missing. Some who claim to have received God's love have missed this huge neighborhood that needs his love.

What is it? It's our neighbors throughout the world. With the global community more and more connected via social media, there's really no excuse now to miss caring for these neighbors. Our neighbors are both local and global.

Consider these astounding facts and realities:

According to a World Bank study in 2010, 1.4 billion people live at or below the poverty line.[1] Most of them exist on less than one dollar a day, the cost of a burger on the dollar menu. Two billion others subsist on less than two dollars a day, less than a cup of Starbuck's coffee.

Let's put it another way: Almost half the world is struggling simply to live. Day to day, they don't know where their food, clothes, water, and shelter will come from.

Thousands of young girls (and some boys) are caught in the quagmire of human sex trafficking. They are kidnapped from their homes and sold into slavery. Some are even sold by their parents as a way to make money to meet their own dire needs.

The young girls most often don't know they are being sold into sex slavery. They think they are going to a city where they can work and send money home to help their parents. When they arrive in the city, they are drugged, and then, over time, become addicts and prostitutes. Their addictions make them totally dependent upon their pimp. Any money that they do make is immediately confiscated by their pimps and not sent home to the parents.

These vulnerable young people are at the disposal of sin-sick men from around the world. Then, as their bodies grow older, they are treated like disposable garbage. New girls are then kidnapped. The cycle continues. It's a multibillion-dollar industry.

These girls are our neighbors. They are God's children created in his image.

Many of the problems faced in today's world are inextricably connected. One problem exacerbates the other. That's the case with sex trafficking and orphans. Many young girls are forced into sex trafficking because they are orphans.

The numbers about orphans are both staggering and startling.

There are an estimated 140 million orphans in the world today.[2] War and genocide are two obvious reasons. Disease causes kids to become orphans as well.

Many of these orphans sell themselves as human slaves in order to eat. Yes, human slavery exists today, as real as that in the colonial South years ago. Moreover, many of the female teenaged orphans end up selling themselves into sex trafficking. They have no food, clothes, or shelter. All they have is their bodies. And they sell them to depraved, godless men.

Here is another real problem throughout the world: In 2015, about 16,000 children under age five died each day.[3] Many die from preventable diseases, mostly caused by unclean water. A well with clean water can give life to hundreds of people in a village for years to come. It's a solvable problem.

Meanwhile, Christians in the western world regularly sing and say to God how much we love Jesus, yet these global neighbors continue to go unnoticed. We do little to nothing to help them.

Do you even care?

You can't ignore them any longer. You can't deafen your ears to their cries any longer. They are there. We do know it. They are our neighbors.

The Value of Short-Term Mission Trips

There is some debate in churches today about the value of short-term missions trips. Some suggest that the cost of the trips doesn't cover the value of people going there. Some say that such trips are nothing more than vacations to a different part of the world shrouded in the word *missions*.

It's a valid question to ask. But if a person's heart is right, and he is truly going to serve in Jesus' name, I would argue that these trips are invaluable. Primarily, they give an eye-opening exposure to the world's conditions. People see firsthand the way most of the world lives. And when they return, they are never the same. They become an advocate for the poor.

Marilynn and I have visited several Syrian refugee camps. We will never forget visiting with a mom and her eight children. Her husband lost his life by a rogue bomb. They fled to Lebanon. They lived in a tent with a few carpets flung on the floor and a central stove pipe. They lived day to day on a few dollars, mostly supplied by churches and relief organizations.

Marilynn and I will never forget what we saw. It's indelibly etched in our souls. It continually fuels our hearts for Syrian and other refugees around the world.

Go on a short-term missions trip to a vulnerable area of the world. You'll never be the same. It is worth every penny you spend to develop a heart for your hurting neighbors around the world.

It will exponentially increase your love for hurting neighbors around the world. And perhaps you can help ignite a similar passion in the hearts of your friends and associates.

The Biblical Perspective

The Bible teaches over and over again about the responsibility that God's people must have toward the poor and needy.

- The people of Israel were commanded throughout the Old Testament to care for the poor, sojourner, and alien (Exodus 23:8).

- In Leviticus 19, the entire chapter is devoted to loving God and neighbor—which is encapsulated in verse 18. Loving your neighbor includes being generous financially to the poor and alien (verses 9-10), not stealing from anyone (verse 11), not being deceptive in any way (verse 11), not oppressing, robbing, or exploiting the poor by paying unfair wages (verse 13), or not showing favor to the rich above the poor in any judicial decisions (verse 15).

- According to Deuteronomy 27:19, a person who doesn't care for the poor is called cursed. Who wants that moniker? God constantly reminded the Jews that they were once a people enslaved without hope. Yet he came to them

in Egypt and rescued them. He told them that the love
he had extended to them should be evidenced by the way
they loved the poor and sojourner in their midst.

Countless other examples about God's heart for the poor could be
added from throughout the law, psalms, and prophets.

The same is true in the New Testament.

- Jesus said that when you care for the "the least of these my
  brothers" you are caring for him. When you look into their
  faces, you should see his face (Matthew 25:31-46).

- When Paul received permission from the Jerusalem Coun-
  cil to take the gospel of grace to the Gentile world (Acts
  15), they made one very strong request. Preach the gospel,
  but don't forget the poor. He assured them he never would
  (Galatians 2:10).

- James gives this clear command in his letter: "Religion that
  is pure and undefiled before God, the Father, is this: to
  visit orphans and widows in their affliction, and to keep
  oneself unstained from the world" (James 1:27).

Christians can never earn God's grace and mercy. God's elective
love is freely given. He first loved us. That's the basis of our great love
for him.

But if you have received his great love, you are to care for your
neighbors, both locally and globally, in response to God's unmerited
favor to you. It's one way to prove your love for the One who first loved
you. It's an acid test that every Christian can take to see if you've rightly
responded to the love you've received from the Father.

I dare you to take the test. Start reflecting on how much of your
time, talent, and treasures are used for you versus how much you
extend to your neighbors—especially the poor among you. See if it's
largely disproportional. I think you'll see how much you love yourself.
That's not necessarily bad. You're just supposed to love your neighbor
as much as you love yourself.

I dare you to pray the most dangerous prayer anyone can pray: *Lord, break my heart for what breaks yours.* I dare you! If you do, and it's prayed sincerely, he will reveal to you what breaks his heart and to where he may be calling you.

Daniel did. As a result, he left his six-figure job. He formed an organization called Beds for Kids. He realized that when street families finally manage to enter apartments, the kids often don't have beds. If they don't sleep well, they can't perform well in school. He now raises money to purchase and deliver beds for kids all over the Charlotte area and beyond.

Hollis did. Her heart was broken for girls caught in sex slavery. As a result, she is now furiously working to help free these girls, find jobs for them, and help give them a future and a hope. She has even gone to Haiti and entered brothels and helped young girls escape the prostitution that has enslaved them.

The McKenzies did. Their hearts were broken for people who had never heard the glorious good news of the gospel. They left their comfortable church jobs and are now seeking God's call for a place where they can share the gospel among the most unreached people in the world.

Might you pray this dangerous prayer as well?

Teach Your Children Well

My own personal passion for caring for the poor has been in my heart for as long as I can remember. From where did it come? Yes, there is something innate within me prompting me to love my neighbor who is poor because the image of God is stamped on my heart and theirs. If it's true that the human race is one, then when I love others, I am showing love to myself. I am connected to a common humanity.

Many secular humanists adamantly feel this same empathy. It's why non-Christians care for others as well.

But I think that it goes much deeper than that for me. It's rooted in my new nature in Jesus. His life within me prompts me to love as he loves. And Jesus' heart is concerned for the poor. Therefore, so must mine be.

I also believe that I received this passion from my dad. After he died, someone sent me an article written about Dad in the *Orlando Sentinel*. For more than 16 years, he was the senior pastor of the First Presbyterian Church of Orlando, Florida. The article was written by Robert Stuart, the executive director of the Christian Service Center for Central Florida, an organization my dad helped found.

Here is the article. It will give you an insight into seeds sown long ago into my heart by my dad about the need to love your neighbors, especially the poor in our midst.

> When I was in high school, many years ago, I confess that often I would sneak out of the pew at the First Baptist Church of Orlando and walk across the street to hear the Rev. Dr. Howard Chadwick at First Presbyterian Church of Orlando.
>
> However, it wasn't for decades that I realized the incredible and lasting impact of Dr. Chadwick and how our lives are forever joined by the legacy he has left.
>
> Dr. Chadwick joined First Presbyterian Church of Orlando in 1966 as its senior pastor. His deep baritone voice epitomized godly leadership, and I decided that's what the voice of God must sound like. I got to know Dr. Chadwick through his son David, then a basketball player for the University of North Carolina, and now a wonderful pastor in his own right. David mentored me as I struggled to have an impact on my team at Edgewater High School.
>
> I share this because just a few weeks ago, Dr. Howard Chadwick, at the age of 91, passed from this life into the next, joining Helen, his wife of 63 years. I am honored to know that one day my own legacy will join his—that left through our work at the Christian Service Center.
>
> In 1971, when Orlando was struggling economically from what we have called the "modern day gold rush," it was Dr. Chadwick who led the downtown pastors to begin thinking beyond their own doors. The Christian Service Center

was established as a place for people who were hurting. In 1975, when men and women were standing on the streets of Orlando looking for food, Dr. Chadwick rekindled this spirit by starting the Center's Daily Bread program.

Dr. Chadwick continued to lead this effort until he retired from First Presbyterian Church in 1982 to help lead other churches as interim pastor in Jacksonville, Winston-Salem and Charlotte.

Now, 38 years later, the center has served hundreds of thousands of families with compassion, food, clothing and financial assistance. Just last year, Daily Bread served its 3 millionth meal—no small task, sparked by a cutting-edge vision.

Dr. Chadwick's recent death announcement said little about the remarkable impact this man had on millions through just one organization here in Central Florida. He left a legacy worthy of honoring and following.

During this time of year, when we count our blessings [the article was written around Thanksgiving] and remember our neighbors in need, let us ask ourselves, what kind of legacy will we leave?

Dr. Howard Chadwick looked into the future and saw a way to help others; may we all strive for such selflessness.[4]

To say I'm proud of my dad would be an understatement. He knew that life was a "So That." He lived so that others could live. The way he proved his love for God was by loving his neighbor—especially the most deprived. He was a great man for many reasons—not the least of which was his commitment to care for the poor.

There's an old song that adjures parents to teach their children well. Parenting is an important calling from God. My personal adjuration to all parents is this: Teach your children well about their need to care for their poor neighbors as they care for themselves. Take them on mission trips. Take them with you as you love the poor in your city. Please build into their hearts my dad's kind of passion for your poor neighbors—both locally and globally. It's an important way you teach them well about your love for Jesus.

That's one of the powerful blessings you can pass on to your children.

Final Thoughts

In a world where people constantly seek fame and incessantly drive themselves to be great, here's yet another way to redefine greatness from God's perspective.

Think about these truths from the Great Commandment:

1. Realize God first loved you. It's an undeserved love. He first recruited you to be on his team.

2. Realize he wants your entire love in return. Loving God with all your heart, soul, mind, and might is an appropriate response to the way he first loved you.

3. Realize you love God most when you love that which he loves the most: humans—especially your neighbors in need—the ones near to us and around the world.

This is the heart of the second part of the greatest commandment. This is what God has done for us. It's all about his greatness and love for you. He is the hero of the story. He is the one who solely deserves all honor and glory.

When you love God with all that is within you, and love your neighbor as you do yourself, you are great in his sight.

And you have moved from superficiality to significance.

QUESTIONS TO PONDER

1. Is it accurate to say that your neighbor is everyone in the world? If so, how?

2. Is your life a "So What?" or a "So That"? If you answered "So That," what difference should that answer make in your life?

3. Can you define gentrification? How has it affected your city?

4. To where have the poor in your city moved? Are they near you?

5. Examine issues like segregated schools and systemic racism in your city. Is there anything you could do to help address these problems? If so, what?

6. What could you do in your city to give someone the hope for upward mobility?

7. Are you aware of the extraordinary suffering that exists in the world? If so, how does this information affect your heart?

8. Who have you cared for recently by your physical presence?

9. What one thing could you do to aid global injustice or poverty?

10. What can you do to teach your children well about the issues of the poor among you?

11. What could you do to help your family better understand God's love for the world?

CHAPTER 7

THE GREAT PERSEVERANCE

I remember once talking to Phil Ford, probably the greatest point guard in the University of North Carolina basketball history. He was highly recruited out of Rocky Mount, North Carolina, as a high school senior. Every major college wanted his basketball services.

After an arduous recruiting season, Phil finally committed to UNC. Everyone thought he would start as a freshman. He was that good.

I asked Phil if Coach Smith ever promised him he'd start as a freshman in the recruiting wars. "No, never!" he immediately responded. "Never once did he do so. In fact, he told me I'd have to compete for the starting position. He said that I was behind all the other guys vying for playing time because I didn't know the system. In fact, all he emphasized was how hard it was going to be."

Indeed, most guys who played at UNC remembered (as I did) Coach Smith honestly saying something like this to them: "You're presently a great player in high school. You dominate your conference. You've obviously got potential or we wouldn't want you at our level. However, everyone you will now play against will be as big, strong, and quick as you are—some even bigger, stronger, and quicker. From day one, you will be elbowed, bruised, and beaten. Practices will be extraordinarily hard. We will be the best-conditioned team in America.

After some of the running drills, you will want to throw up. There will be times you want to quit. You need to know all this before you begin playing for me. If you aren't ready to pay this price, perhaps you shouldn't come be a part of this program."

Coach Smith was a wise leader. He clearly painted a picture of his expectations and what would happen to members of his team. He was brutally honest about what he knew we would face when we committed to his program.

The Cost of Following Jesus

So was Jesus. The night before he was to face the agony of the cross, he said to his disciples in John 16:33: "In this world you will have tribulations. But rejoice, I have overcome the world." He told his "team," his followers, that if they followed him into the world, they would have great tribulations.

"It will not be easy," Jesus was saying. He clearly stated to his followers that they would suffer pain, persecution, and rejection. They would live in a very broken world.

Moreover, Jesus said if his followers unabashedly preach, believe in, submit to, and obey the Word of God they will experience "persecution" arising "on account of the word" (Mark 4:17).

Jesus was honest and told his disciples what they would face.

Paul's Perspective

The apostle Paul understood this truth as well. In fact, he sent Timothy to the church at Thessalonica to encourage them amidst their grave afflictions. He wrote, "You yourselves know that we are destined for this. For when we were with you, we kept telling you beforehand that we were to suffer affliction, just as it has come to pass and just as you know it" (1 Thessalonians 3:3-4).

Paul wanted the Thessalonians to remember that afflictions are expected for those who follow Jesus. He reminded them that they "are destined for this." The Thessalonians had been warned "beforehand" about these tribulations when they chose to follow Jesus. They should have been prepared for them.

Paul said something similar to Timothy as he mentored him: "Indeed, all who desire to live a godly life in Christ Jesus will be persecuted" (2 Timothy 3:12). All means all. *If* you are committed to following Jesus and desiring to live a godly life, trials and tribulations are going to happen. To be forewarned is to be prepared.

Paul also used the analogy of being an athlete to describe someone who decides to follow Jesus (2 Timothy 2:5). Athletes regularly face opponents who want to beat them, sometimes even obliterate and humiliate them. They should understand and be forewarned from the outset that there will be claw marks, deep cuts, bruised bodies, pulled muscles, broken bones, dislocated joints, sprained ankles, and twisted knees. All these things will happen simply by choosing to play in the game.

Coach Smith knew that. So did Jesus and Paul. That's why they were brutally honest about what all would face when choosing to sign the scholarship offer and play in the game.

Counting the Cost

When invited to follow Jesus, people often respond by simply standing or raising their hands. They may even fill out a card. They know their sins are forgiven and subsequently have great joy.

These methodologies aren't necessarily bad. However, they raise a serious question. When tough days come to them; when trials regularly stare them in the face; when the enemy does tempt to kill, steal, and destroy; will they run away from the faith?

If this describes you, I wonder if you were ever told about the great tribulations that Jesus and Paul promised would regularly confront you. I wonder if you thought the Christian faith meant only constant blessings, favor, and prosperity from the Father.

Sometimes I wish evangelists and pastors—when calling people to faith as they raised their hands, or stood, or filled out a card—would also warn them about promised and certain future trials, tribulations, persecution, suffering, and pain, like Coach Smith did his players when we signed our scholarship offers. Like Jesus and Paul did.

Some statistics suggest that as few as 20 percent of those who profess to receive Christ maintain their commitments to him for their entire lives after having decided to follow him. Some even suggest the percentage is lower—especially at large evangelistic rallies. If true, that's startling.

Dietrich Bonhoeffer, the famous German theologian who gave his life for Jesus as he stood against the Nazis in Germany, once said in his book *The Cost of Discipleship*, "When Jesus bids a man to come and follow him, he bids him to come and die."

That's what Jesus was saying to his followers. If they persecuted him, they would certainly persecute them. The pupil is not greater than the master (John 15:20).

Numbers Defining Success?

What is it about numbers defining success in our churches? Why is it so prevalent and consuming in the church?

I understand that people were counted in the New Testament. There were 3,000 saved at Peter's Pentecost sermon. Someone counted 4,000 and 5,000 as the numbers Jesus fed. I understand that numbers aren't unimportant. Like the numbers that come up during a visit with the doctor, they can help measure vital signs and health. But numbers don't show what's occurring inside people. They can't see inside the heart.

Are numbers as important as we Christians make them out to be? We now have the "Top 25 Fastest Growing Churches in America." From where does this come? Is the church now emulating football and basketball polls? Are we now going to have preseason polls that predict which churches will grow the fastest and rank them one to twenty-five?

Moreover, I wonder if the numbers would be as large in these fast-growing churches if people were regularly told about the fierce fires and terrible tribulations Jesus' followers would most assuredly face when they decided to follow him.

I worry that many of these people raised their hands or stood up in a service during an emotional moment. They were taught to expect God's continual blessings. But some time later, they abandoned their faith during difficult circumstances. They didn't realize that tough times would come. They were not sufficiently warned of the inevitable tribulations that come to all who decide to follow Jesus.

Counselors at the church I pastor constantly tell me about a large number of people who professed to have accepted Jesus. Then their supposed faith is severely challenged. Through different messengers, mostly on television, radio, or podcasts, they were convinced their life as a Christian would become easier, a life filled with prosperity and blessing. Then when life's trials persistently continue to come their way, their faith is shipwrecked.

We have had to retrain their brains about Christian discipleship. We've had to tell them what it really means to follow Jesus. We show them what the Bible really teaches about what they can expect as Christians.

After hearing this, many say, "Somehow I missed that." They may not have missed it at all. It may not have been told them.

My friends in Africa, who are leaders in their churches, also bemoan this reality. They tell me that unscrupulous evangelists and faith teachers blow through their nations and promise God's prosperity. People respond in droves. They are poor and need material blessings. But after these faith teachers have left, the prosperity doesn't come. In fact, genocide and persecution often follow people's faith declaration. I'm told that many leave the Christian faith feeling betrayed and forgotten by God. African church leaders have to pick up the pieces and teach the truth of what it truly means to follow Jesus.

Trials come to all of us, yes—especially for Jesus' followers. This truth needs to be taught and known from the first moment a faith declaration about Jesus is made.

The Source of the Trials

From where do these trials come?

First, they come from within you. They are inward struggles built into your fallen, selfish, sinful human nature. They cause a daily battle and struggle with the Holy Spirit, who now resides in you. They are fierce and furious. They won't go away completely until death.

For five years in the late 1990s and 2000s, I was the chaplain to the

Charlotte Hornets' NBA basketball team. Regularly, I would conduct the chapel service for any member of the team who wanted to attend before the game.

During this time, I'd choose a Scripture passage for the players. We'd talk about it for a few minutes. I'd conclude by emphasizing the theme for the evening. Then we'd pray, and the players would leave for final preparations for the game.

One chapel service, I chose the theme of the inward battle all of us face as Christians. To start the discussion, I asked the different players gathered who was the most difficult player they'd ever had to guard.

One of the big guys immediately responded, "Hakeem Olajuwon," the great center for the Houston Rockets. He had more moves around the basket than a break-dancer on steroids. He was a remarkable talent.

Then one of the other players said with a chuckle, "That's easy. Who else? Michael Jordan." All nodded in agreement, heads cast downward, smiling, all probably with a story of a great move they'd either seen Jordan do or had done on them.

Then there was silence. One of the Hornets smiled and looked up at me. It seemed he wanted to say something but wasn't sure he should. I encouraged him to do so. He was one of the Hornets' better defenders. He was also known to be quite confident about his own abilities. Finally, he shrugged his shoulders and simply said, "There ain't nobody I can't guard."

All the other players laughed. His bravado was well-known. What's interesting is that he really did believe there was no one in the league he couldn't guard, Olajuwon and Jordan included.

Then something hit me. This particular player had a history of different issues and problems with his behavior. It would have been terribly inappropriate for me to say what I was thinking. But here's what went through my mind: *There ain't nobody you can't guard? Yes, there is. You can't guard yourself.*

He was unable to discipline the tribulations within himself, the enemy within, his own sin nature.

This enemy within can't be coddled. He must be daily and regularly fought, destroyed, captured, and killed. The Bible says Jesus' followers must crucify the flesh (Galatians 5:24). All who decide to follow Jesus need to be properly warned of this enemy within.

The second source of your tribulations is the world's system of values. It's incessantly trying to mold you into its priorities. It emphasizes self above serving, getting above giving, and power above humility. It saturates the media and every corridor of influence. The Bible adjures you not to be conformed to this world's values, but be transformed by the renewal of your minds (Romans 12:1-2). This too is a constant battle that continues until your last breath.

There's another source of your trials. He is your spiritual enemy and opponent. He constantly strategizes war against your soul. His name is Satan, the devil, or the evil one. He is a formidable foe. His craft and power are great. He is armed with a cruel hatred toward anyone who loves and follows Jesus.

In my decades of walking with Christ, I've learned that this opponent has two major schemes and strategies.

First, he wants people not to come to faith in Jesus at all. He'll devise every strategy possible to keep people from confessing their sins to God and receiving the gift of forgiveness by grace and eternal life through Jesus. He does not want people in heaven.

If that doesn't work, and we do receive Jesus as our Lord and Savior, he moves to his second strategy. He wants you to have hard times—a moral failure, a dark night of the soul, a hurting heart—anything that prompts unbelief so you'll give up. He wants to put you on the sidelines so you can't and won't play.

In athletic terminology, he wants to give you a spiritual ACL (anterior cruciate ligament) injury. If he can't keep you from committing to Jesus' team, then he wants to render you ineffective on Jesus' team. He wants you out of the Christian game. He doesn't play by the rules. He doesn't care if you experience pain. He just wants you sidelined.

The enemy will motivate people to criticize and reject you. Sometimes they will even persecute you (Matthew 5:10). He just wants you to give up your faith and stop playing the Christian game. He wants you to stop pursuing God's will as your master passion in life.

The Key to Victory: Perseverance

In my opinion, the victory over the enemy is found in this key biblical word: *perseverance*. It is an essential word for you to understand to experience victory over the enemy and all the world's tribulations. Perseverance is essential if you want to successfully follow Jesus to the end.

Do you want to be great in the sight of God? Do you want to move from superficiality to significance in your spiritual life? If so, it's necessary to have great perseverance. That's the title of this chapter. It's essential for true greatness and significance. Amidst recurring tribulations, you must continue with great perseverance until victory comes.

The secular world consistently applauds perseverance. For example:

When we hear the story of Winston Churchill, one of the greatest leaders in the Western world, failing in grade school yet still becoming one of Britain's greatest prime ministers, we love his perseverance. He was asked to come back to his grade school and give a speech. During the speech he said, "Never give in, never give in, never, never, never, never—in nothing great or small, large or petty." When we hear this story, we want to applaud his exhortation, don't we?

When we hear that Thomas Edison tried several different ways to invent the alkaline storage battery and he was asked, "Aren't you ready to give up?" and responded, "No, now I know several thousand ways that won't work." Don't you admire his perseverance?

When you hear that Walt Disney was fired from one of his first jobs because, purportedly, he lacked creative, imaginative ideas, you find that incredulous. Yet he refused to quit and became an enormous success in the entertainment industry. Don't you love his perseverance?

When you see a movie about a man hiking in the mountains, getting his arm caught between rocks without hope of escape, after 127 hours, eventually amputating his arm to set himself free, and he now teaches all over the world about never quitting, don't you respect his perseverance?

When you read about William Wilberforce's fight against the slave trade in Britain for decades, him battling through sickness and despair, refusing to give up until finally Parliament voted freedom for all slaves, a vote he heard about on his deathbed, don't you love his perseverance?

The stories could go on and on. Books will continue to be written and movies made of humans who overcome enormous obstacles through the power of perseverance. And people will continue to spend their money to be inspired by them.

Why? It's because there is something within us all that knows the importance of perseverance. We know instinctively how it should be honored and respected. We know it should be a part of our lives as well.

If this is true in the physical world, and obviously it is, wouldn't it also be true in the spiritual world?

For example, think about perseverance and prayer. In Luke 18:1-8, Jesus tells the story of the persistent widow. In verse 1, he gives you the purpose of this story: Don't give up, and keep on praying.

The central character of the story is a powerless bag lady. Some sort of unexplained injustice had been done to her. She wanted justice. So she started banging on the door of the unjust judge. He ignored her. She wouldn't quit. She kept on banging on the door until the judge wearied of her knocking.

Finally, he caved to her demands. She wore him out with her persistent knocking until she got what she felt was just.

Jesus concludes the parable in verse 8 and pointedly asks, "When the Son of Man returns, will he find faith on earth?" Do you hear what he is asking? At his second coming, will he find that his disciples, including you, have persevered through all their tribulations and still believe in him?

Or will you be on the sidelines, nursing your spiritual ACL injury, complaining to God, unwilling to get back on the field and face and conquer your opponent?

Paul said you should rejoice in your tribulations. He wrote that the highway to hope is traversed by the power of perseverance. Tribulations produce proven character. And proven character produces a kind of hope that doesn't disappoint (Romans 5:3-5). But this hope happens only when tribulations first come to your life.

These tribulations must then be met by powerful perseverance.

The Test of Faith

Some through the centuries have called these tribulations "the test of faith." I would argue that Jesus uses your opponent, the evil one, for this test and his purposes. He desires your faith to be strong (Luke 18:8). So he allows the enemy to attack you, to come against you, causing tribulations, to see if your faith is as strong as you say it is.

As a Christian, you recite creedal confessions and tell others of your love for Jesus. Sometimes I think the Lord hears your faith declaration and says, "Well, let's see if your faith is as real and strong as you say it is. Let's test it." Your eternal Coach then permits the enemy to attack you and the test/game to begin.

Let me illustrate. If you heard me say, "I'm a better basketball player than Stephen Curry," what would you do? Yes, I'm certain I'd hear a few snickers. I'd probably hear a lot of belly laughs!

But what if I persisted in saying, "I'm a better basketball player than Stephen Curry"? What if I appeared serious and I kept saying it over and over again, not ceasing to boast of my basketball prowess?

I think you'd not only tire of my boasting, but eventually you'd say to me, "Prove it. Get on the court and prove your claim." You'd be correct in demanding the challenge.

Finally, on the court, we'd all quickly find out if my claims were fantasy or fact. We'd find out if my words met reality.

I think that's how Jesus uses the enemy, Satan, in your life. He allows him to challenge you to see if your words match your life.

Jesus did so with Peter, one of his closest friends and companions.

In the Upper Room, the night before the cross, Jesus predicted that one of his disciples would betray him. All vociferously objected, especially Peter. Apparently his objections drowned out all the others.

Jesus then told Peter that Satan had asked permission to sift him like wheat. He wanted to tear him apart, to viciously hit him, to put him on the sidelines with a spiritual ACL, to take him out of the game.

Note two things here. First, the enemy had to ask for permission from Jesus before attacking. That's because he's merely the prince of this world (John 14:30). By contrast, Jesus claimed to be the King of the universe (John 18:36-37). Satan is a creature. Jesus is the Creator. Satan is on a leash. He can only do to Jesus' "players" what Jesus permits him to do to them. That's why he had to ask Jesus' permission before attacking Peter.

Second, note Jesus granted this permission. He allowed it to happen. It wasn't because of Peter's sin. He did it to test Peter's faith. He said so. He told Peter that after he had persevered through the test and trial and gained victory over it, he was to teach others how to persevere in their faith and gain victory when their great tribulations occur.

Remember This

As you persevere, please don't forget the last part of John 16:33. Even though Jesus clearly warned that all his followers would face tribulations, he added, "But rejoice, I have overcome the world." You are to rejoice in the tribulations because Jesus has overcome the world. If he is in you, and you're abiding in him, that means you too will overcome the tribulations you face.

What does this mean? After many years of following Jesus, here is my answer: God does not necessarily give you an overcoming life; he gives you life as you overcome.

When tribulations come, the strain of perseverance is your strength. If there is no strain, there is no gain. When you take the first step of perseverance, resisting the tribulation, Jesus gives you his overcoming power. The tribulation may seem impossible. It's meant to be so. It seems impossible to all but God. But every decision to persevere gives you God's necessary strength for the next step and the eventual overcoming victory.

As you face the tribulation and choose to resist the problem, Jesus gives you the necessary spiritual strength to persevere and win. It's the important distinction in the Christian life between deliverance *from* trouble versus deliverance *in* trouble.

The first is a false gospel too many have been taught and bought into. The second is faithful, sound, biblical truth. The first causes people to jettison faith in difficult times. The second causes people to persevere with a profound faith that eventually influences the world for Christ.

Faith Declarations

That's why, amidst the tribulations, you should have biblical faith declarations in your spiritual arsenal, ready to be proclaimed over and over again. You live by every word that comes from the mouth of God in his Word. They are to be proclaimed, with dogged perseverance, amidst the trials:

- With the psalmist you say, "I will not be moved!" (Psalm 16:8).

- With Jeremiah you affirm, "The steadfast love of the Lord never ceases; his mercies never come to an end; they are new every morning; great is your faithfulness" (Lamentations 3:22-23).

- With the apostle John you say, "He who lives in me is greater than he who lives in the world" (1 John 4:4).

- With Isaiah you proclaim, "No weapon formed against us will prosper" (Isaiah 54:17).

- With Paul you declare, "I am more than a conqueror through him who loves me" (Romans 8:37).

- With Jesus you state, "All things are possible with God" (Matthew 17:20).

The Enemy Won't Give Up

Even as you make these faith declarations, you must remember that the enemy is relentless. He won't give up. Even after trying to tempt Jesus in the wilderness and losing, he didn't give up. He finally left him, but only "until an opportune time" (Luke 4:13).

Later, the enemy returned and tried to use Peter as his instrument to persuade Jesus not to go to Jerusalem and face the cross. Jesus recognized the wile and the one behind it. "Get behind me, Satan," he said (Matthew 16:23).

Many commentators think the enemy was also present in the Garden of Gethsemane, making one last desperate attempt to persuade Jesus not to go to the cross. Jesus asked the Father if there was a way to avoid drinking the cup of his wrath. He wondered if there was another way for salvation to occur. The enemy must have been behind these thoughts. But Jesus must have realized what was happening in this final temptation. Finally, in faith, he uttered, "Not my will but yours, Father" (Mark 14:36).

As the relentless attacks of the enemy occur, again, remember this truth: Even though he is a serious, smart, and powerful opponent, he's still a creature, not your Creator. He's on a string. Yes, he prowls around like a roaring lion looking for ways to attack and destroy you (1 Peter 5:8). But he can only do to you what Jesus permits.

That will help you to recognize and believe that there is purpose in the pain.

The Victory Is Secure

Jesus has overcome the world. If your life is deeply enmeshed in his, then you too have overcome the world. That means God is causing all things—all tribulations, trials, hurts, messes, problems and pain, everything in your life—to be used for your good and God's glory. This is a promise for all who are called by him and committed to playing life's game according to his plan and purpose (Romans 8:28).

Every follower of Jesus will face great tribulations. Your coach, Jesus, said so. He was honest with you, warning you before you signed on the dotted line to follow him.

Therefore, you shouldn't be surprised when (not if) they come. To be forewarned is to be prepared.

When they do come, and you overcome them with great perseverance, you are great in the sight of God.

And you've moved from superficiality to significance.

QUESTIONS TO PONDER

Here are some questions you can ask to see the strength of perseverance in your life.

1. When you came to faith in Jesus, in what ways were you forewarned that there would be trials, temptations, and tribulations?

2. Did you think the Christian faith was just prosperity and blessing? Why or why not?

3. If you were not rightly taught, how might this warning have better helped you prepare for your faith journey?

4. Can you see how persevering through trials has produced a proven, eternal, Christ-like character in you? If so, how?

5. Can you point to a time when Jesus may have permitted a satanic confrontation/battle/situation to "test your faith"?

6. When this happened, what did you learn about your faith? Did your words about your faith match your life in Christ?

7. Have you used this perseverance that has built your faith to help someone else in his faith walk? If so, how?

8. Can you describe a time when your strain has become your strength? How did it lead to an overcoming faith?

9. Define *perseverance* and *endurance*. Are there people you greatly admire who have persevered through great trials? Who are they? What were some things they did to persevere?

10. Can you describe the difference between deliverance *from* trouble versus deliverance *in* trouble?

11. What does it mean to be "more than a conqueror" (Romans 8:37)?

12. What does 1 John 5:4 mean when it says, "For everyone who has been born of God overcomes the world. And this is the victory that has overcome the world—our faith"?

CHAPTER 8

THE GREAT WANT TO

I didn't get to play a lot my sophomore year at UNC. We had a great team. For the third consecutive year, we made it to the Final Four. We were loaded at the position I played. So I sat on the bench a lot. The joke among my friends was they didn't recognize me walking around campus because I was standing up. I joked back, "Well, I had a better seat than you did!"

At the end of my sophomore year, I had my annual evaluation with Coach Smith. It's something he did with every letterman. He would use this time to evaluate our strengths and weaknesses. He would be brutally honest with someone if he thought he'd never get any more playing time. In fact, with these few, he'd even offer to help them transfer to another school where they might get more playing time.

Several guys who played my position and were ahead of me were graduating. I knew there would most likely be an opportunity for me to get more minutes in my junior year. But I didn't know for sure if I fit into Coach Smith's plans. This meeting would be very important for me to determine what my future might look like.

I went into his office for that fateful meeting with a bit of fear and trepidation. I didn't know how the conversation would go. I decided to take the reins into my own hands and begin the conversation with bold confidence.

"Coach Smith," I said, "next year, I want to play some more minutes. But what I really want to do is to help the team" (I knew this was foremost in his mind as a team-first coach). "Coach," I continued, "how can I help the team win games next year? That's my most fervent desire, to help the team."

He paused for a moment. He looked at me intently. Then he responded. "David, do you really want to help the team next year?" "Oh yes, Coach, that's what I really want to do. I want to help the team." "Well," he continued, "if you want to help the team next season, here's how you can do it: Become a better player."

Then he outlined for me in great specificity how I could become a better player. I needed to work on my foot speed. Become stronger. Be a better rebounder. Then he said what I wanted to hear: "If you do these things, you can help our team. You can get more minutes next season."

Coach Smith also added this caveat: "But if you don't, your playing time will be about what it was this season." He didn't need to explain this further. Clearly I knew how much playing time I had received my sophomore season. I knew what I had to do.

Therefore, I committed myself to a rigorous off-season regimen of very hard physical conditioning. I disciplined myself to lift weights, run, and go to the gym every day to enhance my skills. I knew I needed to work very hard to improve in all those areas Coach Smith had mentioned.

Was it difficult? Yes. Was I motivated? Absolutely. I had a great want to in my heart. I really wanted to be better, quicker, and stronger. I wanted this goal more than anything else in my life.

I devoted countless hours every single day to getting better. I was extremely disciplined. I said no to certain things I knew would hamper or deny this goal to be reached. I said yes to whatever I knew would help me reach this goal.

The Great Want To

Okay, I need to make a confession here. As best I can tell, there is no stated "great want to" in the Bible, church history, or Christian theology. I confess it's a term I made up.

Would you give me just a little latitude on this one?

Why? Because it makes my point. My great want to in basketball guided me to the success I knew at UNC and beyond. It was an essential ingredient for success.

Similarly, in the Christian life, there must be a great want to regarding a specific desire Jesus has for all his followers: holiness.

It's not something a lot of people these days desire more than anything else. But in God's eyes it is not optional. It's his passionate yearning for all who follow him.

The Bible commands God's people: "Be holy; for I am holy" (Leviticus 19:2; 1 Peter 1:16). That's God's desire for you. That's his purpose for every person whose life is in Christ. God's end goal for you is not happiness, nor health, nor prosperity, nor success, but holiness.

Did you know that the only adjective used in triplicate in the Bible to describe God is the word *holy*? The angels, before God's mercy seat in heaven, cried out, "Holy, holy, holy, is the LORD of hosts" (Isaiah 6:3).

It could be easily argued that the two primary characteristics of God are his love and holiness. These two major characteristics of God are at the heart of the gospel. His holiness is what's offended and shattered by your sin. His love is what motivated the sending of his Son and your Savior, Jesus, to die on the cross for the forgiveness of your sin so your relationship with God could be restored.

What does the word *holiness* mean? It describes someone or something that is different or set apart. When God, who is holy, captures your heart, there is a great want to for difference from the norms and values of the godless culture in which you live. It's a call to purity. It's being in the world but not of the world. It's a fervent passion to be like God. It's a consuming desire to be conformed to his image.

Paul says that the ultimate goal of Christians should be to become conformed to the image of Jesus (Romans 8:29). When the Holy Spirit enters your heart, he begins the slow but sure process of shaving off godlessness and replacing it with the life of Jesus.

It begins in the heart. The heart of the matter is a matter of the heart.

That which fuels this holiness is the great want to. It's the follower of Jesus' fervent desire to be like him.

An Example from My Kids

I have three children. They are a primary source of joy in my life. I love them beyond what words can express.

At one time or another, I've said to each of them: "I want to tell you how pleased I am with all you've accomplished. It's wonderful to see the way you've used the different gifts God has given to you. But what I'm most pleased about is that you've chosen to follow the Lord Jesus as I've chosen to follow him. There is no better way you could choose to honor me than to love and obey the Lord I love and obey."

I have witnessed each one of my children deciding to follow Jesus and then choosing to live for him. This choice to be different in a dark world has brought extraordinary joy to me. They are living the life their dad chose to live. They have chosen holiness as their father has chosen holiness.

Above any academic, athletic, worldly success, they have chosen to be different as I chose to be different. They have desired what I wanted most from them—to be conformed to the image of Jesus.

It is your Father in heaven's desire for you as well. The greatest gift you can give back to him is your desire to be like him. Your most fervent passion should be to emulate his life and be conformed to the image of his Son and your Savior (Romans 8:29).

You do so when you want to be holy as he is holy.

An Example from Marriage

In my opinion, this is one of the major reasons many marriages are failing today, even among Christians. You've wrongfully bought the lie that your marriage partner was given to you to make you happy and fulfill all the longings of your heart.

What a lie! No person can complete another. In Ephesians 5:26, a verse that compares the marriage relationship to Jesus' relationship with the church, Paul writes his desire that Jesus "might present the church to himself in splendor, without spot or wrinkle or any such thing, that she might be holy and without blemish."

Jesus' work in both the church and marriage is to present a person as holy to the Father in heaven.

I've learned, albeit sometimes painfully, that my marriage is where I most glaringly see the ugliness of my sin. It's a graduate school of learning about my selfish nature. My relationship with Marilynn constantly shows me how far short I am of Jesus' servant heart and his perfect holiness, and how gross my self-righteousness can be.

Instead of Marilynn completing me, our marriage shows my supreme selfishness and lack of holiness. It's only when I let Jesus complete me in his holiness can I begin to be what Marilynn needs from me.

Life coaches constantly adjure people to write down end goals they want to accomplish in life. Their clients are often asked to make a bucket list of all they want to do before they die. Some of these goals are noble and honorable.

But here's my question to you: Does your list ever include holiness? It should. If your goals in your life don't include holiness, I am certain that your passion for God will atrophy. Nature abhors a vacuum. False idols will surely enter your heart and quickly push holiness aside.

A primary goal God desires for the person who wants playing time on his team is a great desire to be made holy.

When the New Birth Occurs

I'm often asked how I've seen the church and Christian teaching change over the 30-plus years I've been a pastor. I regularly give the same answer. When I first started teaching, the gospel that ministers preached was focused on the glory of God and what you can do to serve him. Now, more and more, I hear Christian teachers talking primarily about my needs and what God can do for me.

God is *not* an endless blessing machine for his people (though I do believe he is a giver of good gifts). The gospel of Jesus Christ is not about you. It's about God. He didn't save you so he can be your eternal sugar daddy. He came to save you so that you would become a holy person who can help change an unholy world into his image.

The gospel of Jesus Christ is about God putting you back into a perfect union life with him. There is no longer any sin separating you from God. Any sin in your life separates you from God and sullies the relationship. It must be removed.

God takes your sin and gives you his righteousness forever. Your heart is made new. You're not guilty anymore. You're not filthy in his sight anymore. You are a new creation. The old has passed away. New life has come to you. When God looks into your heart, he only sees his perfect, holy righteousness (2 Corinthians 5:16).

Moreover, God's *Holy* Spirit injects his holiness into your soul at the moment of the new birth. Then, over time, the process of sanctification (the process of being made holy) starts to spread into every area of your life. It won't be completed until you get to heaven. But holiness is undeniably happening to you from the moment of the new birth.

In a sense, you could compare this to what cancer does to the human body. There is a primary tumor in the heart, the lungs, the brain, or some other place. Over time, it gradually metastasizes and advances all through the body. Eventually, the body dies.

When it comes to the new birth, the primary tumor is in the heart. It is converted, changed, and made healthy. This new health, or holiness, starts to spread to every other part of your life, leading to a new life of eternal health and holiness.

For the rest of your life, this great want to, the desire to be holy, is always present. You want to keep your feet, hands, tongue, and thoughts holy before your holy God. You desire to obey his moral law—not because you have to but because you want to. It's a joy to do his will (Psalm 119:14).

Your passion for every detail of your life passionately wants to be under the scrutiny of a holy God. You desire to please him above all else. Holiness is the natural affection of what God has done for you in Christ. You want to behave according to who you now are in him.

You want to be holy as he is holy.

What You Must Hate

For holiness to happen, there must also be a hatred of sin in your life. Without this, a desire for holiness will forever seem to elude you.

God hates sin. You must as well.

This need for hatred of sin became real to me in a childhood experience.

One evening my mom fixed dinner. As a part of the meal, she fixed some beets. Previously, I had eaten beets without incident or problems. They weren't my favorite or least favorite food. Mom prepared them; I ate them. I thought they were healthy for me. At least that's what she regularly told me.

This one night was different. From the moment I ingested those beets, my stomach began to dance a dance of denial. It did not want those beets in my system. It began a violent rebellion. A fever ensued. I went to bed immediately and rushed to the bathroom about every 15 minutes, throwing up what I'd eaten. My nausea was relentless throughout the night.

Mom was there by my side all night long, placing a cold cloth on my forehead. She was very concerned, wondering if she should rush me to the emergency room. Was it food poisoning? She'd never seen me so sick. It lasted into the next day.

Finally, mercifully, the fever and the pain abated and eventually ceased. My stomach calmed down. Slowly but surely, strength returned to my body.

That happened decades ago.

Yet something significant has happened to me internally from that moment onward to this day.

If someone puts a beet on my plate, I become nauseous. No kidding! If I even smell a beet, I start getting sick to my stomach. My kids incessantly tease me about it. Marilynn immediately scrapes them off any salad brought to us at a restaurant before it's divided among us.

Because of this experience, I hate beets. It's not a mild annoyance. It's a virulent, violent, and negative reaction. I can't go near them. I won't go near them. Even as I write this paragraph, when thinking about beets, I'm feeling a bit nauseous.

This incident has given me an important insight into holiness. To be a holy person, you must hate sin. You can't merely put up with it. You can't coddle or snuggle up to it. You must hate it. If you even get near it, your heart should immediately become sick.

You then instantly remember the hurt this sin once caused you. You immediately and negatively react to the pain it inflicted on you. This painful memory motivates you never to go near the sin again.

Sin destroys. To overcome and conquer the destruction, you must despise the sin that previously enslaved you.

This hatred of sin is closely akin to a word in the Christian vocabulary that is increasingly MIA (missing in action): repentance. Jesus began his ministry by preaching, "Repent, for the kingdom of heaven is at hand" (Matthew 3:2). The word "repent" was important to him. It should be for us as well.

What is repentance? The best definition I've ever heard is "Stop it!" You love Jesus so much that you stop doing the sin that breaks his heart. You hate the power of sin reigning in your life and want it gone. You know you can't love Jesus and keep doing what he hates. You know you have to repent of sin before you enter his kingdom.

Repentance is the natural byproduct of hating sin.

I hated the lack of playing time I experienced as a sophomore at UNC. The thought of sitting one more season on the bench made me sick. At one point, I even thought about transferring to another school so I could play more. That's how much I hated the idea of not playing that next season.

Do you see my point? My great want to in order to play more minutes was fueled by my hatred of sitting on the bench. Both needed to be present for me to have success.

That's the key to overcoming sin and achieving holiness. You must hate the sin and what it's done to you. You repent and leave it in your past. But you must also love something more than you love the sin.

Think about the love stories that capture your heart. There's an addict who falls passionately in love with a virtuous woman. Over time, his love for her is so great that he eventually gives up the addiction to spend a lifetime of love with her. His love for her is more powerful than his desire to sin. Over time, he becomes like she is. He is holy as she is holy.

That's the great want to.

You choose to repent of every destructive hurt, habit, or hang-up because of the great grace you know that Jesus has given to you on the cross. You desire to be conformed to his image. You know that God's will for you is holiness.

It becomes a fervent passion, your greatest want to in life.

Connecting Holiness and Obedience

Scripture tells us that holiness and obedience are inextricably connected. Jesus said, "If you love me, you'll obey my commandments" (John 14:15).

My great want to with Coach Smith to play more my junior season was linked to obeying what he told me to do: Get bigger, stronger, and faster. If I didn't obey him, I wouldn't receive more playing time. If I did, I would play more.

In the 1980s, I had the privilege of meeting a pastor of one of the largest churches in the world. As a young pastor, I was intrigued to know why he was successful. One of my friends was able to arrange a dinner with him where I was able to sit next to him.

He was polite and engaging. We had a warm conversation. Finally, I got up the nerve to ask him the question I had wanted to ask him.

"Would you mind telling me the secret to your ministry success? What is your secret?"

He giggled in a way I still remember today. Then he giggled again. "You want to know the secret to my success?" he said. "Oh yes, please," I answered.

Then he responded with these simple words: "I pray and I obey."

He prayed and obeyed. He prayed. But he also had the great want to. He desired above all else to be holy. He desired above all else to obey God's will in his life.

He prayed and obeyed.

Examine your desire for obedience. Look at your heart and discern what motivates your actions. You must have a heart that is truly loyal to God. Obedience brings us near to God.

It increases holiness.

The Obedience of Grace

Obedience is necessary for the success of the soldier or athlete (2 Timothy 2:3-7). They know the importance of being under authority. They must learn how to live and learn how to do so without questioning or complaining.

Obedience is faith in action. When you obey, it proves you trust the one giving you the commands.

Obedience is also the acid test of love. Jesus said, "Whoever has my commandments and keeps them, he it is who loves me" (John 14:21).

God's commands are always issued to his followers because he loves us. God's moral law is good, righteous, and holy (Romans 7:9). His commands are never given in tyranny, but for your best interests and good. They are founded in God's perfect righteousness and justice. They are his good guardrails to protect your life from going into the ditch.

Therefore, God's grace should motivate obedience. And your great want to, the desire within to obey God's will at all costs, should produce a life of holiness.

A Few Personal Tips

Here are a few tips I've learned through the years about garnering and guarding God's holiness in your life. Others taught them to me. I hope they help you as well.

First, there is no such thing as sinless perfection in this life for the follower of Jesus. First John 1:8 clearly states that if you say you never sin as a Christian you are lying. In this life, even after the new birth, you still have a sinful nature not totally yielded to Christ. Every Christian still sins—sometimes willingly, and sometimes unwittingly.

When you do sin, you should immediately know it's wrong and want it removed from your life. You hate it. You repent. It's like beets to you. It sickens your heart. You have the great want to in your heart to rid yourself of anything that causes you to be unholy.

Many Christians call this process of spiritual growth *progressive sanctification*. It means you're not as bad as you were yesterday and you're not as good as you will be tomorrow. But you're getting better. You're becoming more holy every day. You're being conformed to Jesus' image every day you live.

Most every college basketball coach I know says that the largest jump in becoming a better player occurs between the freshman and sophomore years. But they also tell me that a serious athlete should be getting better every day he plays the game.

Similarly, every day, month, and year the Christian should be becoming more like Jesus. Why? It's because the great want to drives you toward holiness.

Yes, there will always be setbacks. The world's values and your selfish nature will keep trying to woo you back into a life of degradation. The devil, your mortal enemy, will never tire in his temptations to godlessness. He forever wants you to return to a life focused on self.

But that's not what you want. You want to be holy, as God is holy.

Second, when you do fail, practice 1 John 1:9. It states that when you confess your sins, he is faithful and just and forgives you of all unrighteousness. You go back to the cross of Christ. You receive grace anew. After having received this fathomless grace, the great want to increases even more.

God's never-ending, amazing grace inspires holiness. His unlimited love motivates obedience.

Third, don't use 1 John 1:9 as an excuse to sin. Again, when you confess your sin, God is faithful and just to forgive you of all unrighteousness. God does forgive all sin.

Just make sure you never use God's boundless grace to continue in your sin. That's abusing God's grace. It makes a mockery of the meaning of the cross.

In fact, 1 John 3:16 suggests that if you are in Christ and habitually sin, you are a liar. You are kidding yourself. A continually sinning Christian is an oxymoron. It's impossible. If you do this, it only proves you've never actually received and experienced the new birth in Christ and his profound love.

Fourth, after you've sinned and you've received God's forgiving grace, remind yourself of a principle that a professional golfer once told me: "The most important shot in golf is the next one." You play life's game with a short memory. The past is the past. You leave it behind and press on toward Christ (Philippians 3:13). You refuse to drive your life's car staring at the rearview mirror. Doing that only causes more accidents. The most important moment in the life of a Christian living under grace is the next one. The most important day in the life of a Christian living under grace is the next one.

Fifth, claim Philippians 1:6: "He who began a good work in you will bring it to completion." Jesus will complete the task of holiness, of perfectly conforming you to his image. It's his job to do it. It won't be completed until heaven. But it will happen. God will do it. Rest in this powerful promise.

Sixth, learn from your failures. Indeed, make failure your friend. You may have failed, but you are not a failure. Your identity in Christ is always secure (John 10:28-29). You realize too how failure can actually enhance holiness. You now know how not to do something. You better realize life's traps and temptations. You now order your steps daily not to step in that mess again. You're more prepared for future attacks, temptations, and assaults.

God's Goal

Holiness is God's goal for every Christ-follower. It's not optional. It needs to become your passion and goal for your life in Christ.

And holiness is best motivated and achieved by the great want to. The most fervent desire in your heart, and your life's most fervent passion, should be this: Be holy as God is holy.

When you greatly want to be holy as God is holy, God is greatly pleased.

You're considered great in his sight.

And you move from superficiality to significance.

QUESTIONS TO PONDER

1. Do you want holiness more than anything else in your life? What evidence is there of that desire?

2. Do you live life looking constantly to your past, regretting what you did? Or have you truly discovered grace and recognized that God has forgiven your past and given you a new life for today and tomorrow?

3. Do you hate sin? When you see something inappropriate on television, a movie, or in a book, or hear a dirty joke from another person, does your stomach churn because this is unholy and hurts the heart of God? Do you want to turn it off, stop reading it, or refuse to listen to it?

4. When you are reading or watching something godless and unholy, do you ever imagine Jesus sitting next to you? Do you ever imagine what he is speaking to your heart as you are placing this filth in your mind? What is he saying?

5. Does sin that has hurt you in the past make you nauseous? Does your heart hurt when you think about your past? The people you've hurt? The ways your sin has hurt your own life?

6. Is there a distinct difference between your life and the world and its values? Describe that difference.

7. Define repentance. How have you repented in your life? What sins have you hated?

8. As a Christian, you have been called out of darkness into Jesus' marvelous new light. What changes can others see in you because of Jesus Christ in your life? Or is your holiness hidden?

9. Do you ever use God's grace as an excuse to continue to sin? When confronted with sin, do you whisper to yourself, "Oh, I'll be forgiven"? and then keep on sinning? Why does this make a mockery of the cross?

10. How do you handle a backward step, a failure in your desire for holiness?

11. Do you see the progression of holiness that has occurred in your life? Are you holier than you were a year ago? Would the people closest to you note your changes in holiness?

12. Do you believe that you've committed a past sin that is beyond the grace of Jesus? Why or why not?

13. What does it mean to be conformed to the image of Jesus? Is this a description of you? Why or why not?

14. Describe ways you can daily experience the amazing love of God that dwarfs all your sin.

15. What are some examples of the traps the evil one will use to keep you from being holy? What plans do you have to prevent the traps from ensnaring you?

CHAPTER 9

A GREAT GENEROSITY

I was in Iowa City, Iowa, with my wife Marilynn. We were watching our son Michael swim in the 2015 NCAA championships.

Out of nowhere, a text arrived from a friend in Charlotte. He congratulated me on the check Coach Smith had sent to all his former lettermen. I didn't have a clue what he was talking about. I dismissed it.

Then my cell phone rang. It was another friend in Charlotte who asked me about the check from Coach Smith. I asked him to explain. He went on to tell me that Coach Smith had written in his will that every one of his former lettermen would receive $200 from his estate after his death. He simply wanted all of us to go out to dinner on him.

When I arrived home from Iowa, sure enough, the check had arrived. A note from the estate's trustee told us to enjoy the meal on Coach Smith.

Coach Smith practiced great generosity. Even from eternity he generously reached back to members of his basketball family. Even from the grave he wanted us to remember that it is more blessed to give than to receive. From eternity he wanted us all to remember that life is far more about giving than getting.

He knew the importance of generosity being a part of a life lived well.

Visiting the Doctor

When you go to the doctor for your annual checkup, the first thing the nurse does is check your vital signs. You are weighed to make sure your weight is generally the same as the year before. Your temperature is taken to check for a fever. Your blood pressure is measured to see if it's in the safe range. Your heartbeat is monitored as well.

All this is essential for knowing if you are physically healthy.

Similarly, God is concerned about vital signs connected to your spiritual health. One of the major ones is your attitude toward money. Most people are constantly preoccupied about it. Perhaps you worry about whether you have enough now and for retirement. Will you be able to pay for the kids' college education? You're anxious if you blew too much on that risky investment. You wish you had more, but you also remember Jesus' incessant warnings about the danger money poses. You are reminded that more than half of his parables deal with the subject of money. You know it's God's chief rival (Matthew 6:24).

You know the importance of contentment. You realize you need to silence the inner voice that incessantly cries out, "You need more." Paul learned contentment while in prison of all places (Philippians 4:11). He knew what it was like to have a lot and little. He found freedom when Jesus alone became the master passion of his life.

Yes, Paul had to learn contentment. It probably took some time. I imagine it took a long time to learn it. But he did learn it.

You know you should learn it as well.

Paul said to his mentee, Timothy, that godliness with contentment is great gain (1 Timothy 6:6). When you think about all the things in life you want, do you include godliness with contentment? I think it's at the heart of practicing great generosity.

Spiritual health is directly connected to generosity. The word *give* is mentioned more than 2000 times in the Bible—far more than *faith* or *love*. The essence of God is his generous giving. After all, he gave no less than his own Son because he loved you (John 3:16).

By the way, after the nurse finishes with all the numerical measurements, she leaves. You then wait for the doctor to arrive. When he does, he begins his check-up.

What does the doctor commence doing? He starts pushing and probing in different spots all over your body. If he pushes in a place and you say, "Ouch," a concerned look may cross the doctor's face. He might say, "Uh-oh, it's not supposed to hurt there."

The Great Physician, Jesus, does similar kinds of checkups on you as well. Yes, he pokes and prods your spiritual life in the area of financial generosity. When you know you are selfish and stingy, you should say, "Ouch!" God, the greatest giver of all, then says, "Uh-oh, it's not supposed to hurt there."

God's people are called to great generosity. It's not optional.

From the Beginning

When God first began the work of salvation, he called Abraham. He promised him that he'd be extraordinarily blessed. Through his seed, more people would be touched than the stars in the sky or sand on the seashore.

God gave Abraham one condition about this promise. God reminded him that he was being blessed in order to be a blessing to the world (Genesis 12:3). In short, he was being blessed to be a blessing.

From the first moment that God formed the covenant with Abraham, he gave the reminder that great generosity was a vital sign of good spiritual health. Abraham was never to forget that blessings are to be given away, not hoarded.

I recently returned from a missions trip to Haiti. This tiny nation is still reeling from the devastation of the 7.0 earthquake of 2010. Right after I returned, Hurricane Matthew blew through Haiti and sucker punched Haiti again. Terrible poverty grew even worse.

As I walked around and noticed the dire poverty, I gasped with sadness. I couldn't help but ask myself, *Why not me? Why wasn't I born here in Haiti? Why was I born with all the advantages I've been able to enjoy as an American citizen?*

These questions partly paralyzed my soul. Admittedly, I felt some guilt. That is, until I remembered Genesis 12:3. If God has blessed me, it is for one primary reason: to be a blessing to others.

I then recommitted myself to doing as much as possible to help poor Haitians and rebuild their nation.

Do We Understand?

I wonder: Has this message been grasped in the American church? For example, the average American Christian purportedly gives away approximately three percent of his income. Thirty-seven percent of those who call themselves evangelical Christians don't give anything away. The average American Protestant parishioner gives around $17 per week.[1]

How can this be? Especially when you know the Bible's clear instructions.

It forces all of us to come to grips with this uncomfortable reality: We spend much more on ourselves than we do on others. It appears American Christians are not content. It seems that we constantly want more and more.

Great generosity seems to be missing in action for many American Christians. We are blessed, but it appears we are not blessing others anywhere near as much as we could be.

Fundamentals of Generosity

For us to move toward greater generosity, there are three fundamentals that must be understood. You must train your brain to believe them. It is a discipline of the mind. Behavior follows belief. Without these fundamentals, you will never be content and you will never be a blessing to others.

You will never practice great generosity.

What are these fundamentals? The first one is that God owns everything. This is his world and he created it. "The earth is the LORD's and the fullness thereof" (Psalm 24:1). He offers us the privilege of living in his creation. But it's his world.

That means that everything you have in this world is a gift from God. *Everything!* Every breath you take, every morsel of food you ingest, every piece of clothing you place on your body, every relationship you enjoy, and all the money you have—everything is a gift from God.

Yes, you may have worked hard for your money and possessions. But even your ability to work hard is a gift from God. Who gave you your body and mind? Who gave you your natural talents? Who placed within you the energy that's in your body? God did all this (Deuteronomy 8:18). They are his gifts to you. How you use them is your gift to God.

Everything we possess flows from the gracious hand of a loving God. He owns it all. This is the first and necessary fundamental for you to believe if you want to be set free from the bondage of money.

That leads to the second fundamental: If God owns everything, then he has loaned it to you for however many years you live on this planet. You are expected to wisely oversee *his* possessions that *he* has loaned you. You are to use them for *his* glory. You are to be a partaker of his divine nature by being a great giver.

You are not to use his possessions that he has loaned you to hoard more and more for yourself. You are to learn contentment. You are to find your sufficiency in Jesus and him alone. You then find ways to use his possessions for his glory by giving to others. That's the definition of a steward: someone who faithfully oversees another's possessions.

Yes, enjoy God's blessings that he has given to you. Material possessions aren't bad. He creates all things to be richly enjoyed (1 Timothy 6:17).

Just always remember that you are blessed to be a blessing. Live life with an open palm. Don't hold onto anything in this world too tightly. That's how God began the covenant with Abraham. He wants all people everywhere to understand this truth.

Jesus tried to teach these two fundamentals over and over again. In several of his parables, there is a boss who owns everything. He then departs and leaves his possessions in the hands of certain managers and workers. They clearly know that it's a loan from the boss. And they are to be good stewards of *his* possessions.

Then Jesus gave the uncomfortable third fundamental. It's the kicker that causes uneasiness. It's the zinger that coerces discomfort.

What is it? Jesus said that one day he will return and hold everyone accountable for how they have rightly or wrongly overseen his possessions. He even suggested some rather harsh judgments and treatments for those who practiced irresponsible stewardship.

Most every great leader knows that people don't do what you *expect* but what you *inspect*. Jesus will practice this great leadership principle when he one day returns to earth and holds everyone responsible for how they have overseen his possessions that he loaned to them.

Do these three fundamentals cause a bit of a tremor in your soul? They should. God is God. You are not God. And most of your problems come when you get that point confused. These three fundamentals should cause a pause within you. They are the foundation for learning contentment and practicing great generosity.

It's all God's money. You are called to be his money manager with what he has loaned to you. And you will one day be held accountable for how you've used his money. Are you using it for his glory?

Gods wants his people to live to give.

Four Practical Steps

Do you want great generosity in your life? If so, here are four practical steps you can take to become a great giver. They have worked for many. They have worked for me. When rightly practiced, they will allow you to be a blessing to others and generously manage God's resources he has loaned you until he returns again.

All four steps are found in the wisdom material in the biblical book called Proverbs. Solomon learned these truths. You would be wise to do so as well.

1. Make a Realistic Budget

Live within your life parameters and means. Don't look at what your neighbor or friend possesses. That's a major source of discontentment. Look only at the amount of money you have coming in and live off that budget.

A budget is you telling your money how it's going to work for you, not your money telling you how you will work for it.

Here is what Solomon wrote:

> A sensible man watches for problems ahead and prepares
> to meet them. The simpleton never looks and suffers the
> consequences (Proverbs 27:12 TLB).

Know well the condition of your flocks, and give attention to your herds (Proverbs 27:23).

The plans of the diligent lead surely to abundance, but everyone who is hasty comes only to poverty (Proverbs 21:5).

Jesus echoed these same truths. He said that you should estimate the cost before building a tower. Otherwise, people may vociferously ridicule you when the tower isn't completed (Luke 14:28-30).

Of course, Jesus was addressing the need to count the cost of discipleship before deciding to follow him. He wanted his followers to know up front that following him could cost them their prestige, influence, and even their life. But I think he's also talking about day-to-day living. He's talking about the need to live within one's means.

American marketing and media commercials will constantly try to tell you that you need more of something. They want to create a covetous, discontented heart. They want to prompt you to buy the lie that somehow you are missing something in life if you don't have certain products.

To defeat these promptings, you need to make a budget. Your budget will then tell your money how it will be used, instead of the culture telling you how you should spend your money. Your budget will silence the voice of *more* from the culture.

This important first step sets the course toward contentment.

2. Be Free from Debt

Someone once said that money talks. I agree. It incessantly says, "Bye-bye!" And it most often leaves your hands and goes elsewhere because of debt.

Carefully read this from the pen of Solomon: "The rich rules over the poor. And the borrower is the slave of the lender" (Proverbs 22:7). When you are in debt to someone or an institution, you are a slave. They have authority over you.

How? If the God of the universe has prompted your heart to give to a need somewhere, you must first timidly approach the god of debt and ask permission to give to bless others. That's why Jesus said that the chief rival god to God is money (Matthew 6:24). Both have a spiritual, invisible power. Both try to woo you to worship and obedience. But you cannot serve both. It's impossible. Only one will rule you.

Paul said that you should owe no one anything except the debt of love (Romans 13:8). As you love your neighbor, there should be a strong desire to reciprocate that love. That's what Paul was referring to. He wants Christians to love others so much that there's a debt of love to be reciprocated. That's an acceptable kind of debt.

The culture's way of exacerbating debt is convincing you that you need more and you need it now. Many such messages flood your mind daily. You become convinced that contentment in life is just one purchase away.

I love this joke: Who is more content—the man with $10 million, or the man with 10 children? It's the man with 10 children because he doesn't want any more.

Resist the culture's lies. Tear up your credit cards and their 18 per-cent debt repayment plans. Are you aware that people pay 47 percent more at a fast-food restaurant with a credit card than with cash? It's called hunger buying. You do the same thing in grocery stores if you are shopping while hungry. You think you are hungrier than you really are. So you buy more.

If needed, get professional advice to help you pay off your debts. Many churches have programs that can assist you. You can get them online. More and more secular offerings are available. Just furiously and relentlessly attack and slay the debt monster. It may take time. You may have to do it slowly. But just do it! Find the smallest debt first. Then pay it off. Experience a small victory. That will show you it can be done. Then attack the next one. Then go after the next one. As some-one once said, "Inch by inch, life's a cinch."

Also, most of your creditors will work with you as you work through your debt. They don't want you to declare bankruptcy. They'd much rather receive something than nothing at all.

You can get out of debt. It leads to financial freedom, contentment, and the ability to practice great generosity.

3. Start Practicing Wise Savings

Many people don't. They think about and live solely for today.

There's little thought of tomorrow. In fact, 76 percent of Americans are living paycheck to paycheck.[2] For some, there is no other choice. Sadly, systemic poverty is alive and well in America.

But there are many people who, because of their financial choices, are enslaved to living only for today with no thought of tomorrow. Solomon challenged the folly of not thinking about tomorrow:

> Precious treasure and oil are in a wise man's dwelling, but a foolish man devours it (Proverbs 21:20).

> Wealth gained hastily will dwindle, but whoever gathers little by little will increase it (Proverbs 13:11).

Talk with investors about a savings plan. Many people don't sign up for their company's plan because they are too lazy. Do you really think the government will take care of you? Predictions say that Social Security will run out of money in the next decade or so. The nation's debt presently stands in excess of $19 trillion. It simply can't be sustained.

Practice wise saving. Look at it as a gift you will be giving to yourself. In the later years of life, you'll be glad you did this.

4. Practice Generous Giving

Here is what Marilynn and I have done from day one of our marriage. We have tithed 10 percent of our income to the local church we are a part of. It's off the top, no questions asked. We believe the truths of Malachi 3:8-10. The first 10 percent belongs to God. It's what he taught his chosen people, the Jews (Leviticus 27:30). When it's not practiced, as Malachi said, we are robbing God. Why would God bless a thief?

Moreover, Marilynn and I believe the tithe is the starting point for generous giving. It's God's training wheels for learning generosity. It seems to be where God started with the Jews. I'd think that's where he would start with Christians as well.

But Marilynn and I have not stopped with the tithe. We believe great generosity includes tithes *and* offerings. We believe the New Testament's perspective on grace giving is where Jesus wants his followers to be. Therefore, we do practice the tithe. That's the starting point.

But wouldn't God want followers of Jesus' generosity to exceed the Law? So we started practicing a double tithe. It took a few years to get there. But we did it. The first 10 percent goes to the church we are a part of. The second 10 percent goes to wherever the Holy Spirit leads our hearts to give.

In fact, over the years, we've tried to increase our giving to exceed the double tithe. It's been fun to do so. It's the primary way we have learned great generosity and how to break the back of the money monster.

Jesus' model for generosity was the widow in Mark 12:41-44. He was in the temple courtyard. People were bringing their offerings. The rich religious leaders would often make a show of their giving. Sometimes they'd even hire trumpeters to blow their horns before they gave. This would draw attention from onlookers so they could show off the large amounts they were giving. (By the way, I heard someone suggest that this is from where we get the phrase, "Tooting your own horn.")

A poor widow arrived in the courtyard to give her gift. She made no show of her giving—a mere two copper coins. But Jesus saw the amount. More importantly, he noticed the heart behind the gift. The religious leaders gave out of their abundance, but it didn't affect their lifestyles one bit.

But the widow gave from her meager paucity. It *did* affect how she lived. It was sacrificial. She gave up something for God's glory. Therefore, it was considered a generous gift to God because it came from the little she possessed.

Jesus was impressed with her heart. He told his followers that the widow was the one who had practiced great generosity, not the religious leaders. Her example would be the one noted throughout history as an example of generous giving. She foreshadowed the greatest sacrificial gift: Jesus' death on the cross.

Do you want to practice great generosity? Begin with the tithe. It's 10 percent off the top.

I believe that Jesus taught it. He told the Pharisees that they tithed on everything they received, "as you should" (Matthew 23:23). For me, those three words from Jesus express his view on tithing. But he also reminded them that it was far more important to care about the weightier matters of justice and mercy than obeying every part of the law.

But Jesus *did* say that his followers should tithe. I think it's because he knew it would help begin to teach generosity. Moreover, why would Christians, under grace, give less than a faithful Jew living under the Law?

You don't think you can tithe? Well, if you were to suddenly lose 10 percent of your income, how would you adjust? What would you remove from your budget to make ends meet? Do that same exercise now. Then start practicing the tithe.

In Malachi 3:8-10, God promised to open the windows of heaven if you will trust him with the tithe. It's the only place in the Bible where God ever challenges his people to test him. All the other places in the Bible, God tests us—mostly in the area of our faith. But here God calls out his insidious opponent—unbelief. He invites you to test him and see if he won't open the windows of heaven with unimaginable blessings and miracles.

During our first year of marriage, Marilynn had an opportunity to go to a friend's wedding in West Virginia. We were living in Houston, Texas, at the time. There was just one prohibitive problem. We didn't make much money, and we had committed to tithing to our church.

Marilynn's friend wasn't a Christian, and Marilynn wanted to go and be a witness to her and her other non-Christian friends from college. But the money just wasn't there. We were tempted to use the tithe. We felt we could justify it this once. But we didn't feel a peace about doing that. The Bible says the tithe belongs to God and his church. We didn't want to rob God (Malachi 3:8). So we decided against her going.

That next week, after having made this decision, Marilynn received a phone call from Southern Bell in Atlanta, where she had worked the year before she married me. They told her their records said they owed her some money. Marilynn checked her records and told them they didn't. They insisted they were correct. Marilynn insisted they weren't. Finally, they just said, "Could we please just send you the money and get this off our books?"

Marilynn finally relented.

The check arrived two days later by snail mail. Stunningly, it was for the exact amount for a round-trip plane ticket from Houston to West Virginia. Did I note for you that it was the exact amount—to the penny?

Over the years of our marriage, I could tell you many other stories like this one since we chose to practice tithing. We've seen evidence after evidence of God's miraculous provision for us. The windows of heaven have truly opened for us.

Paul's Counsel

Paul's exhortation about grace giving and moving beyond the tithe is found in 2 Corinthians 9:6. In challenging a wealthy Corinthian church to give money to poor Jews caught in the middle of a severe famine, he said to them, "If you sow sparingly, you will reap sparingly. If you sow abundantly, you will reap abundantly."

Paul used an illustration from farming. If you throw only a couple of seeds on the ground, don't expect a large harvest. Contrarily, if you throw thousands of seeds on the ground, expect a large harvest.

That's a beautiful picture of the challenge to move beyond the tithe to grace giving. Perhaps you could gradually increase your giving from 10 to 11 percent in one year. Then go from 11 to 12 percent the next year. As your salary increases, as much as possible, keep your lifestyle the same and increase your generosity. It's another way of shouting *NO* to the culture about impulse buying, debt accruement, and the need for more and more.

It's also a tangible way to keep scattering more and more seeds so you can reap more and more seeds—so that you can continue to generously scatter more and more seeds for God's glory and purposes.

It's a way to practice blessed to be a blessing.

Jesus convicted my heart again about the need to practice grace giving when I was given the privilege of writing books. When I signed the contract with Harvest House to write three books, they offered me a generous advance. I was thankful for the opportunity to write. But, honestly, I also thought it'd be fun to have some extra money and do some fun stuff with my family.

Then the Lord spoke clearly to me. He told me to give it all away.

My first response was, "Are you sure? It takes a lot of energy to write a book. And I'm going to write three!" But he assured me he wanted me to do it.

So I signed over the entire advance and future royalties to a missions organization trying to reach unreached people in India. The advance has planted hundreds of churches all over India where people have never heard the name of Jesus. I believe this act of obedience made Jesus' heart sing.

Guess what? My heart sings as well with joy and contentment when I think about giving his money away. The Lord continues to meet my every need. And he has graciously given enough for me to continue to do fun stuff with my family.

How to Give the Grace Gift?

With your continued learning about grace giving, study the needs of the world. Find out the places where extreme deprivation occurs. Sadly, that is true about many places all over the world—locally and globally. Constantly pray, "Lord, break my heart for what breaks yours." Choose to live more simply so that others may simply live. Listen intently for the Holy Spirit's promptings regarding where his money that he has loaned you can go to help others.

I hope you've now begun to understand the Abrahamic Covenant's meaning that you are blessed to be a blessing. You are not blessed to hoard and have more. You are blessed to be content with what you have and practice great generosity.

One other thought: Make sure you leave a will. Fifty-five percent of Americans don't have one.[3] What's the major reason they don't? Many think that if they do, they'll die.

Yes, you will die. It's a proven statistic. One out of one do. But most likely you will not die immediately after you make out your will. Think of making out a will as your way of gifting the people you love most in the world. Don't leave them here fighting for your assets. Make it clear where you want your money and possessions to go.

Perhaps you can contribute to your grandkids' education. Or maybe you leave most or all of it to a missions organization. In doing this, you not only ensure your kids of having a strong work ethic, but you continue to fulfill God's mandate to take the gospel to all the nations after you're in heaven. I personally believe Jesus would be pleased with this as well.

This will allow you to practice great generosity after your death.

That's what Coach Smith did for his former lettermen.

Final Thoughts

Someone once joked, "God loves a cheerful giver, but he will take money from a grump." I guess that could be true. But I think God would much prefer you be a cheerful giver.

In fact, Paul was the one who adjured you to be a cheerful giver (see 2 Corinthians 9:6-7). The word "cheerful" comes from the Greek word *hilaros*. That's the word from which we get *hilarious*. God loves a hilarious giver. He wants our giving to be overflowing with joy.

I guess God would accept money from a grump. After all, in Moses' day, he plundered the pagan Egyptians' resources for the sake of his chosen people, the Jews. But I'm convinced he would much prefer his children be joyful, contented, and hilarious givers.

That kind of giver understands grace.

He also understands great generosity.

And he has moved from superficiality to significance.

QUESTIONS TO PONDER

Here are some questions for you to consider to see if you have great generosity:

1. Would God call you a generous giver? Why or why not?

2. Do you believe God owns everything in the world and you are a mere steward of *his* possessions that he has loaned you? In what ways could you point to this being true?

3. How are you rightly managing the resources God has loaned you? How might you be mismanaging his resources?

4. What percentage of your total income do you give away? What is your attitude when you do this?

5. Do you practice tithing? Why or why not?

6. Have you tried to move beyond the tithe? Why or why not?

7. How has God miraculously and supernaturally opened the windows of heaven for you as you've become more financially generous? (Keep in mind that his blessings are not necessarily material ones—his blessings are spiritual too.)

8. In what ways have you fallen prey to the culture's lies about contentment and needing more?

9. What is your debt load? What steps have you taken (or can you take) to eliminate it?

10. How have you done with your savings account? What can you do to make sure it continues to grow?

11. Do you have a will? Does your will include giving money to causes that fulfill the Great Commission? If not, why not?

12. Do you desire great generosity in your life? What steps can you take to grow more in this area?

CHAPTER 10

THE GREAT GO

During my sophomore year at UNC, we played in the Holiday Festival Tournament in New York City at Madison Square Garden. Our first game was against St. John's University. We both were ranked in the top ten in the country.

The first half was intense and physical, a back-and-forth basketball game. One thing became increasingly clear during the first half: The referees continually made questionable calls against us. Our frontcourt players accumulated foul after foul.

In response to the foul problem, Coach Smith walked down the bench, trying to figure out whom he should put into the game. He tapped the shoulders of several reserves to help rescue foul-plagued starters.

With about four minutes to go in the first half, yet another whistle blew and another foul was called on one of our big guys. The law of diminishing returns hit. There weren't a lot of other options.

Coach Smith looked at me. Might he put me in the game? It was an important game. I hadn't played much that season. But the foul problems continued to pile up. There was no other place for Coach Smith to turn. It was now my turn.

He tapped me on the shoulder and said, "Go into the game."

I began taking off my warm-ups. There were about four minutes left in the first half. I jogged to the scorer's desk. Someone committed a foul. The buzzer sounded. The referee saw me at the scorer's table. He signaled me to enter the game.

At that moment, I had a life-altering decision to make. I could walk across the floor, go into the locker room, take off my UNC uniform, pack my bags, and take the next plane home to Orlando, Florida, and never play basketball again. Or...

I could go into the game and play.

Leaving the Garden and going home and never playing basketball again really wasn't an option. I had made a commitment and signed a scholarship to play basketball at UNC. I'd given my word. Plus, I really loved playing the game of basketball.

This left me only one alternative: I had to go into the game.

I wish I could tell you I turned the game around in UNC's favor. I didn't do anything spectacular or embarrassing. I played the rest of the half. I did my best.

In the end, we lost a very close game. But it did set the stage for me playing more minutes later in my college basketball career.

Here's the most important truth I took away from that moment in Madison Square Garden. My career would have never moved forward if I didn't do the most important thing I did that evening in Madison Square Garden: Go into the game. I obeyed Coach Smith's "Great Go."

If you are under a coach's authority, you do what he tells you to do.

The Importance of Last Words

My dad died several years ago. His body simply wore out. He was ready to go be with Jesus, his Lord and Savior. Those last several weeks were agonizing for me. I was saying good-bye to someone I truly loved and respected.

I made a special point during those last few weeks to pay attention to whatever he told me. I knew his last words would be his most important words to me. I remember most of them to this day.

Last words express what's most important to a person.

Jesus' last words to his earthly disciples are written down in Matthew

28:19-20: "Go therefore and make disciples of all nations, baptizing them in the name of the Father and of the Son and of the Holy Spirit, teaching them to observe all that I have commanded you. And behold, I am with you always to the end of the age."

These words are commonly called the Great Commission. I think they could also be named the Great Go.

Jesus commanded his followers to go into the game and play. It's not optional. The world is your court. The game is to make disciples of all the nations. If Jesus is your coach and you're on his team, you were created to go into the game. You were recruited, equipped, taught, and prepared to play. You were called to go into the world, not sit on the bench.

If you don't go, you aren't on his team. In my mind, it's that simple. If I didn't go into the game when Coach Smith demanded me to do so, I was no longer a member of his basketball team.

It's God's "Great Go."

How Fragile Life Is

Once you're in the game, you have your marching orders: to make disciples. We're not called merely to get people to make decisions. Certainly that's the first step in making a disciple. A person needs to make a decision regarding who Jesus is.

I do understand this imperative. Every person's eternity is at stake. I understand that no one is guaranteed tomorrow. We've been given an evangelism imperative. Life is a vapor, a mist. It is extremely fragile. It can be snuffed out in an instant.

This became very clear to me years ago. I was not yet married. I was in graduate school at the University of Florida. My parents still lived in Orlando, Florida. They had an opportunity to spend a long weekend in the mountains of North Carolina.

They called me and asked if I'd be willing to come home and spend the night in the house. They felt things would be a bit safer if someone was there. I didn't hesitate. It would give me an opportunity to see some friends, get away from the graduate grind, and get some much-needed sleep.

On the Friday night of the weekend, I slept downstairs in their bed. It was much bigger than mine upstairs. My almost six-foot-eight-inch frame could really get some restful sleep in their bed.

Around 3:00 a.m., I heard some noises outside the door. The light in the bedroom suddenly flicked on and off. Startled, I raised myself on my elbows to see if I was just dreaming. The light flicked on and off again. This time I was able to see a gun about six inches from my head. A gruff voice growled, "Lie down, on your back. Put the pillows over your head. Don't move or you're a dead man." I did exactly what he said to do.

I could then tell that the lights in the room went on for good. I recognized another voice in the room, then another outside the room. They cut the phone lines. Then they tied me up with them, my hands behind my back and my feet at the end of the bed. Obviously, I was unable to move at all.

For the next 45 minutes, they ransacked the house. Occasionally, one of the men would come back to the bedroom to check on me. Most often, he would simply poke the gun in my ribs and remind me not to move or say anything. He reminded me several times that he wouldn't think twice about killing me.

One time he reentered the bedroom and asked me where the drugs were. I told him we had no drugs in the house. He berated me, telling me he saw envelopes with my dad's name on them: "Dr. Howard Chadwick." I told him my dad was a minister, not a physician. Finally, I think he believed me.

Another time, he came into the bedroom and told me they had found my North Carolina watches and rings. My sophomore year we had gone to the Final Four and I had a ring and watch commemorating that success. My senior year we had won the NIT championship in New York City when it was still a very prestigious post-season tournament. Similarly, a championship diamond ring and watch had been awarded each member of the team. "This stuff must mean a lot to you," he said gruffly. "Yes," I said, "it does. It means a lot to me." "We won't take it," he said.

I wondered, under the pillows, if there might be a kind place in their hearts? Was the image of God stamped on them in such a way that even while robbing my parents' house and possessions, they might show a morsel of mercy?

Eventually, there was complete silence. No drawers banging closed. No doors being opened and shut. No more shoes shuffling on the floor. No more hushed whispers. Just silence.

When I thought it was safe, I wiggled the pillows off with my head. I swung my feet over the side of the bed, my hands still tied behind my back. I jumped over to the phone on the wall in the kitchen, hoping they'd not severed the cord on that phone. They had not.

I knocked the phone off the holder with my chin. Then I got on the floor and dialed my sister's number with my hands behind my back. She lived in Orlando and would be able to come over quickly, I thought to myself. I also dialed 911. With both calls, to my sister and the operator, I had to place my face right next to the receiver, begging for help.

Within minutes the police arrived; my sister Carolyn a few minutes after them. They cut me free and began questioning me about what had happened. Slowly but surely I recounted everything that had just occurred that evening.

The criminals have never been caught. I'd hoped my rings and watches were left behind. They were not. They had lied to me about not stealing them. I had hoped they might later show up at a local pawn store. They never did.

It took me several weeks to get over the trauma of almost dying. But as painful as it was, it did something very powerful within my soul, something that has lasted all my life to this moment.

I realized my own life could have easily been taken in a moment. It showed me the brevity of life. It showed me how we're not guaranteed tomorrow. We do need to share Christ with as many people as possible until we die or until he comes again.

This experience awakened within me a passion to share Jesus. There is an evangelism imperative for all Christ followers to go into the game—now.

You need to know the gospel. You need to be able to present it. You need to be sensitive to anyone in your neighborhood or around the world where your coach may be calling you to get into the game. You need to be ready, each and every day, for divine encounters with people the Lord may bring into your path.

The greatest joy I've ever known is leading someone into an eternal relationship with Jesus. My heart ignites with excitement whenever anyone thanks me for his eternal security.

To whom can you point that you've led to Christ? Who will be in heaven because you entered the game and shared the gospel?

It's the necessary first step in making a disciple.

The Next Steps

But that's just the first step. After someone makes a decision, you are to make a disciple. After the decision to receive Christ, people need to take the next step in discipleship: Baptism as evidence of this commitment to their new head coach, Jesus. We are to be "baptizing them in the name of the Father, Son, and Holy Spirit."

It's an important next step.

My wife Marilynn and I were asked to speak in Ethiopia in the 1990s, right after communist rule had been overthrown. For years the church of Jesus Christ had been pushed underground.

Amazingly, we discovered people weren't persecuted for decisions for Christ. Nor were they persecuted for praying, worshiping, reading their Bibles, and serving others in Jesus' name.

Persecution began only when a new Christian was baptized. Before baptism, they would throw up their hands, renounce Satan and their old life, and pledge total and complete allegiance to Jesus.

Only then did persecution begin. That's because the Communist government determined baptism to be the defining public statement of commitment.

That's what Jesus intended baptism to be. It is supposed to be the expression of complete commitment to Jesus. It drives a public stake in the ground. This act uncompromisingly says, "I have decided to follow Jesus, no turning back."

However, as important as baptism should be, the decision to follow Jesus, as expressed by baptism, is only the next step in becoming a disciple. It follows making a decision to follow Jesus. There are a couple more steps.

Remember Jesus' command was to "go" and "make disciples." In fact, the word "disciple" means "pupil, student." New converts need to learn what Jesus has taught us: "All that I have commanded you to do," he said.

Here I think of all Coach Smith commanded us to do. I remember one practice at the beginning of a season when he took a basketball in his hands and said, "Gentlemen, this is a basketball." We all looked quizzically at one another, wondering what he was getting at. Of course we knew it was a basketball! We all had been playing basketball for years.

Coach Smith was reminding us of the fundamentals of the game. For the next couple of weeks, we spent most of the preseason going over the fundamentals of how the game should be played: passing, cutting, rebounding, shooting, screening, etc. Over and over again, he reemphasized how he wanted the game to be played, especially emphasizing fundamentals.

Coach Smith wanted us to remember all that he had taught us. He didn't recruit us simply to make a decision to attend the University of North Carolina. Once signed, he wanted to make us into great players. The decision was just the starting point. He was training us to go into the game.

He was making us into his disciples.

Mentoring

There is another insight Coach Smith gave me into discipleship. Not only did he make disciples of his players, but he also mentored coaches who played for him. The "Dean Smith" coaching tree is all over American and international sports.

Many of his former players and assistant coaches now coach in the NBA, in other colleges and universities, and in high school and middle schools in America. Some even coach internationally, overseeing the teams of different countries.

Then you add the number of college, high school, or middle school coaches who didn't play for him but would come sit in his office and ask questions for hours. Moreover, add all those who came to his clinics during the offseason to learn from him. Only eternity can reveal the thousands of "disciples" he made and mentored in his coaching life.

As I examine the American Christian church, especially after 30-plus years of ministry, it seems to me that we are fascinated with decisions and not disciples. We count our attendance and number of baptisms. It makes individual churches and pastors look great. But have these decisions and baptisms become disciples? Have we responsibly mentored them?

I know and see so many Christians who say they've been believers for years, but seem to still be playing in the kiddie pool. What would you think if you saw a thirty-year-old man sloshing and playing in a kiddie pool? I can't speak for you, but I'd think the guy was not mentally healthy.

Yet many American Christians have never moved beyond their decision. They don't know and practice all the fundamentals of the faith after having entered the game.

From Jesus' perspective, faith becomes real when you get into the game. He wants his followers to reproduce your life in another person. And you don't reproduce what you do. You reproduce who you are.

We are called to mentor others with the faith we have.

We are called to make disciples.

Basketball and My Son

For example, my basketball acumen took on a new dimension in my life when my son started taking an interest in the game. When I started teaching him all the fundamentals Coach Smith had taught me, basketball became a new thrill for me. I was "making a disciple" of my son in basketball. I was mentoring him.

David became an all-state basketball player. He went on to become a Division I college basketball scholarship awardee himself. It was so much fun to see him play the way I was taught to play the game.

One day, I laughed inwardly with delight as I watched my son work a basketball camp for young kids. There he was, teaching those kids all the things that Coach Smith had taught me that I had taught him. If he ever has a son who loves to play basketball, I'm certain—absolutely certain—he will pass on the fundamentals I taught him.

That was Jesus' desire and design for all who followed him: disciples who make disciples who make disciples. It was his job description for all who follow him. Long before Amway ever conceived and made a science of the multi-marketing scheme, Jesus did. It's not rocket science. Nor is it optional.

It's the call to all who follow Jesus. It's how Paul said Timothy should disciple others: Older men training younger men what they had learned (1 Timothy 2:12). It's how the knowledge of one generation is passed on to the next one. It's common sense.

How?

Some may respond here, "But I don't know how to disciple someone. I don't know enough." Then learn.

More specifically, I would encourage you to do the following:

First, learn how to share the gospel of grace with another. It's outlined in chapter 1 of this book, "The Great Exchange." Try to help him make a decision to follow Jesus.

Then I'd encourage you to learn the basic fundamentals of the faith. They are outlined in the ten chapters in this book. It's a major reason I wrote this book. I wanted to give followers of Jesus a way to help mentor and disciple people who want to faithfully follow him.

The next step would be to practice these fundamentals daily and regularly in your own life. Make sure they are an important part of your Christian walk. Write down stories of how each fundamental has helped your Christian growth.

Now find someone who wants to grow and be a disciple of Jesus. Perhaps he is someone you've led to Christ. Or maybe it's a person you know who just doesn't know much. After you have found him, start teaching. You already know much more than he does.

And what do you do if he asks you a question and you don't know the answer? First, it's okay to say, "I don't know." Then go find the answer. In the age of Google, most answers can be found with the pressing of a key. Also, there are many great study Bibles available. Most have extensive footnotes that explain verses, doctrine, context, and application.

Then, when you learn the answer, you've grown in your own discipleship while helping someone else. You learn as you mentor. It's a win/win.

Eventually, after a time of spiritual growth, this new disciple then finds someone else into whom he can build his life. And the process continues until Jesus returns. That was his model—it's not about defining success by amassing large numbers. This may make pastors and churches look great, but it neuters and sterilizes the true power of the gospel of grace.

A legend is told of Jesus' ascension to heaven. He met all the angels. They applauded his return. They were overjoyed with his accomplishment. They worshiped and adored him. They were very proud to be on his "team."

Finally, one of the angels purportedly asked him, "Lord, what is next for the human race? You've accomplished a truly great work. What will happen next for the redemption of all humanity? How will your message continue to grow?"

Jesus responded, "You see those twelve guys down there?" The angels looked down to earth and nodded. "Well," Jesus continued, "I built my life into them for three years. I placed my life in them through my indwelling Holy Spirit. I told them to go into the world and reproduce who I am in them in other people. Then those people, in turn, will do the same. It will ripple outward to all nations for thousands of years until I return. That's how the world will know my grace, kindness, power, and truth."

The angels nodded. Then they looked down at the twelve, a group of ragtag, mostly uneducated, impulsive, and stiff-necked guys. Then they looked back at Jesus. Then back at the twelve.

Quizzically, one of the angels finally asked Jesus, "What's plan B?"

Jesus answered, "There is no plan B."

There is no plan "B." There is only one plan from Jesus. It's to make disciples who will make disciples who will make disciples who will make disciples until he returns. We're called to go into the game. We're called to make disciples.

There's no plan "B."

The Ends of the Earth

In Matthew 28:19-20, Jesus said to make disciples of all the nations. In Acts 1:8, he said his disciples are to be his witnesses to "the ends of the earth." In Mark 13:10, Jesus reiterated that taking the gospel to all the nations is an imperative and a priority for his followers. He also stipulated that he won't come back until every tribe and ethnicity has heard the gospel (Matthew 24:14).

The job remains incomplete.

Over the last few years, Jesus has convicted my heart about this reality. In response, I've committed myself to do everything I can to be faithful to this part of the Great Go.

Think about this truth: Two millennia after Jesus' command to take his gospel to all the nations, there are still more than two billion people worldwide who do not know him. Yes, some have rejected the gospel. But most have never heard it.

For example, in India alone, there are presently a staggering 400,000,000 people who have never heard the name of Jesus. They hopelessly worship idols that cannot move on their behalf and meet the deepest longings of their heart. In response to this reality, over the last several years, Forest Hill Church has planted over 5,000 churches in areas of India where people have never heard.

In Nepal, there are 22 unreached people groups in the Himalayas. Young girls are often taken from their villages and sold into sex trafficking. Forest Hill Church has partnered to try and reach these people with the message of Jesus' love and forgiveness.

In the Middle East, where millions don't believe in the gospel, people are regularly seeing dreams and visions of Jesus. ISIS has forced Muslims to ask why they follow a religion of death and destruction. Muslims today are open to the gospel like never before. Forest Hill Church is now partnering with different outreach ministries to bring the gospel to them.

There are many other places throughout the world where people are trying to present the gospel to those who've never heard. The leadership at Forest Hill keeps asking the Lord, "Where else?"

Are you asking this question? Is your church? How can you not as a follower of Jesus?

Several years ago, I prayed one of the most dangerous prayers any follower of Jesus can pray. I asked, "Lord, break my heart for what breaks yours." The reality that there were so many who had never heard the gospel began to break my heart.

Forest Hill and I became committed to reaching the unreached. We developed a passion for the ends of the earth, those nations that have never heard. We researched and searched for places, people, and nations that needed the gospel. Then we have done what we can do.

We have set aside a significant portion of our budget to take the gospel to these places. Jesus said that where you spend your money shows where your heart is. Therefore, the annual budget reflects this priority and passion.

Also, our annual Christmas Eve offering is devoted to those who have never heard the gospel. Over the last few years, we have raised nearly $2 million. Christmas has become an anticipated season during which Forest Hill people are eager to see where the next offering will go. As God sent his Son into the world, we use this season to remind all that we too are to be sent into the world.

And people have also come to realize that though they may not be able to go physically, when they send their money, they are sending themselves. They are indeed going into the game. They are developing the Great Go in their hearts.

And, yes, when possible, mission teams are sent to these areas. This is valuable. Nothing creates passion in a Christian's heart for the world like seeing the gospel reaching a group of people who had never previously heard.

It Begins in the Home

Parents need to be reminded that making disciples for the world begins with their children. Parents are the primary Christian educators of their kids. Here are some helpful tips my wife and I used with our kids.

First, look for every possible opportunity to share the gospel with them. My wife Marilynn brought all three of our kids to faith while driving around in our van. Talk about a captive audience! We affectionately nicknamed this time "e-VAN-gelism." We minimized social media and gadgets during this time to motivate conversation. It was amazing how all three kids began spiritual conversations with their mom.

We designed teaching moments. Every Saturday night, we would read a Bible story with the kids. Often they'd act it out. We taught tithing, giving each one a dollar in ten dimes and making sure they set one aside to place in the offering the next day. We created an environment in which they were free to ask questions.

We also took advantage of time with them over meals. There is an abundance of sociological information available about the value of families eating together. And don't forget bedtimes. Right before they go to sleep, they are exceedingly vulnerable to deep, meaningful, and spiritual conversations.

Finally, we took them with us on ministry trips. When we'd go serve in fragile places in our community, they'd go with us. When we'd travel internationally to share the gospel, they'd sometimes go with us. They knew Jesus' commands were to take the gospel to the ends of the earth.

My wife and I believe that the most meaningful aspects of faith are caught, not taught. When kids see their parents live out their faith in a passionate and meaningful way, they will want what they have. They will yearn to live out what they have seen.

They will desire to become passionate followers of Jesus like their parents are.

And develop a heart for those who have never heard.

It's Not Optional

This passion to make disciples needs to be in the hearts of all Jesus' followers. It should be both local and global.

He said so. It's a command from the eternal Coach who has called you to play on his team. It's not optional.

It's called the Great Commission. I call it the Great Go.
It doesn't matter what you call it. Just do it. Just go. Get in the game.
It's another way to be "great" in the sight of God.
And to move you from superficiality to significance.

QUESTIONS TO PONDER

Here are some questions I regularly ask myself to make sure Jesus' Great Go is forever in the forefront of my life. I hope they help you as well.

1. Have you shared your faith with anyone recently?

2. Are you praying for the Lord to bring someone to you with whom you can share the gospel?

3. Do you really understand the brevity of life?

4. Do you really believe people who die without Jesus face an eternity without him?

5. In whom are you presently investing your life?

6. How are you making a disciple of someone who can then make a disciple of someone else?

7. Do you have a heart for world missions?

8. How much money have you given to fulfill this part of the Great Go?

9. Do you believe that when you send your hard-earned money you are sending yourself?

10. Do you know where the largest unreached people's group lives—people who have never heard the name of Jesus? (Answer: India.)

11. Do you know where else in the world are large concentrations of people who have never heard the gospel? Can you list them? Have you invested any of your monetary resources to help reach these people?

THE BIG FUNDAMENTAL

Y ou can either play at the game or you can play the game." I've never forgotten those words spoken forcefully to me from one of my basketball coaches. I'd just begun playing the game. My height and coordination had shown some promise. But he'd detected a superficial interest in me toward the game.

This coach then challenged me to move from superficiality to significance if I was serious about playing the game of basketball.

I've wanted to say the same thing to numerous Christians through the years. They seem to be playing at the game of following Jesus. They aren't playing the game the way Jesus desires his followers to play it. There often appears to be a superficiality of commitment, discipline, and practice when following Jesus in their lives.

My college basketball coach, Dean Smith, was a fanatic about fundamentals. Though his teams regularly possessed high school All-Americans and superstars, every year he would take each player on the team through the fundamentals. He knew his teams wouldn't be successful unless they faithfully performed correct techniques in dribbling, shooting, defense, rebounding, cutting, pivots, and passing.

My senior season at North Carolina, Coach Smith knew that the basketball pundits had predicted we'd finish at the bottom of the

Atlantic Coast Conference. No one thought we'd be very good—except for Coach Smith. He saw potential in the team. But he also knew what needed to happen for this team to be successful: We had to be fundamentally strong.

Coach Smith then told us how we would repeatedly perform all the game's basic fundamentals over the next six weeks leading up to the beginning of the season. And we did—over and over and over again—ad nauseam.

By the way, that team was very successful and finished in the top 10 in the country.

Jesus has fundamentals as well. To faithfully follow him, Christians need to repeat them over and over again. When done, they stop playing at the Christian game. They play the game the way he desires.

They faithfully follow him.

They understand what greatness is in God's sight.

They move from superficiality to significance.

What are those fundamentals? I've outlined them in this book. Here they are:

1. *The Great Exchange.* Christians understand the gospel of grace and the power of the cross. They train their brain to understand this truth. They preach the gospel to themselves so they can daily know the Father's love. The Great Exchange is the heart of their faith and the passion of their lives.

2. *A Great Faith.* Christians believe that nothing is impossible for God. They trust God's Word and promises to be true. They want Jesus to notice and acknowledge their great faith as they face any and all life situations. They know powerful prayer is rooted in great faith. They see God at work in their lives—sometimes miraculously.

3. *The Great Reversal.* Christians realize that humility should always be chosen over pride. In heaven, the first will be last and the last first. The first in line will have chosen humility

and serving. The last in the line will have chosen pride and being served. Christians yearn to be at the front of heaven's line. Therefore, they humble themselves in the sight of the Lord and reject all self-exaltation. They then trust he will lift them up.

4. *The Great Paradox.* Christians know that when they are weak, God is strong. They know that the sufficiency of grace can only occur when their hearts are deeply rooted and solely dependent on Jesus. This dependence comes when they have reached the end of their own strength and solely trust in Jesus.

5. *The Great Commandment (Part 1).* Christians know the most important of all the commandments is to love God with all their heart, soul, mind, and might. There is nothing of greater importance. This is the greatest commandment of them all. It's what develops a heart of worship. It's rooted in the reality that God first loved us. Before we ever chose him, he first chose us.

6. *The Great Commandment (Part 2).* Christians know when the greatest commandment of loving God is rightly in place and practiced, the second part of the commandment will naturally follow—loving their neighbor. That neighbor is local and global. It's the primary way we express our love for God, who first loved us.

7. *The Great Perseverance.* Christians know that life will have obstacles and trials. Jesus said so. But they persevere through all of them, knowing that Jesus is using them for his eternal purposes and their good. Perseverance produces proven character; and proven character produces a hope that does not disappoint.

8. *The Great Want To.* Christians desire holiness in their character. The only place in the Bible where an adjective about God is used in triplicate is Isaiah 6. In this chapter,

God is described as "holy" three times. Jesus' followers are
called to be holy as God is holy. They want to repent of
anything that hurts the heart of God.

9. *A Great Generosity.* Christians want to be givers, not takers.
They desire to be generous, not stingy. They know that
God has been generous to them—especially in the giving
of his Son for eternal life. They know the dangerous power
of money to be worshiped as a rival god to God. They also
know the best way to break the back of the money monster
is to give it away.

10. *The Great Go.* Christians are called to go into the world and
make disciples of all the nations. Jesus commanded it. Plus,
they are to mentor the next generation to faithfully follow
Jesus. They are called to be disciples who make disciples
who can make disciples of the next generation.

Jesus wants these ten fundamentals grounded into the daily lives
of his followers. They are not optional. In whatever situation believers may find themselves, Jesus wants them to repeatedly practice these
fundamentals. It's what causes the victorious Christian life to occur.

Tim Duncan is perhaps the greatest power forward ever to play the
game of basketball. His peers and pundits nicknamed this seven-foot
behemoth "The Big Fundamental." That's because every part of his
game was fundamentally strong and accurate. He excellently practiced
every single one—dribbling, passing, rebounding, footwork, defense,
shooting—throughout his great career.

Bottom line: Tim Duncan played the game of basketball the way
it's supposed to be played. Thus the nickname "The Big Fundamental."

In my opinion, Jesus could be similarly called "The Big Fundamental." Every part of his life was fundamentally accurate. He too excellently practiced every single one of these ten fundamentals every day of
his life. He played life's game the way it's supposed to be lived.

Jesus calls his people to follow him. He faithfully practiced these
fundamentals in his own life. His followers should imitate him.

I am convinced that Jesus would like all of his followers to be called "The Big Fundamental" as well.

In one of my basketball games at North Carolina, I played exceptionally well. I practiced all the fundamentals well. My mistakes were few. I graded out as having played as well as I could have played. UNC won the game as well.

After having watched the game films, right before the next practice was to begin, Coach Smith approached me, put his arm around me, and pointedly said, "You played a great game. You played the game the way it's supposed to be played."

Upon hearing this compliment, my heart jumped with joy and I felt extremely satisfied. One of the game's greatest coaches had told me I'd played a great game. As a basketball player, it doesn't get any better than that.

At the end of your life, you will appear before Jesus. The great Coach of the universe will have analyzed your life's game films. He will have graded out how you played.

Try to be as honest as possible. Will Jesus say to you that you played a great game? Will he remark how faithful you were in practicing his fundamentals? Will he tell you that you played the Christian game the way it's supposed to be played?

That's my master passion in life. That's why I wrote this book. I hope it's yours as well.

When you've faithfully followed Jesus and practiced his fundamentals, you're no longer playing at the game, but you are playing the game.

You are truly great in God's eyes.

And you have moved from superficiality to significance.

NOTES

Chapter 3—The Great Reversal

1. E.M. Bounds, *The Classic Collection on Prayer* (Alachua, FL: Bridge-Logos, 2001), 103.

Chapter 6—The Great Commandment, Part 2

1. "World Bank Updates Poverty Estimates for the Developing World, February 17, 2010, http://econ.worldbank.org/external/default/main?theSitePK=469382&contentMDK=21882162&menuPK=476752&pagePK=64165401&piPK=64165026.

2. "Worldwide Children's Statistics," SOS Children's Villages USA, http://www.sos-usa.org/our-impact/childrens-statistics.

3. "Worldwide Children's Statistics."

4. Published November 26, 2009 in the *Orlando Sentinel*. Used with permission.

Chapter 9—A Great Generosity

1. These statistics are from healthfundingresearch.org.

2. Angela Johnson, "76% of Americans are living paycheck-to-paycheck," *CNN Money* (June 24, 2013), http://money.cnn.com. 2013/06/24/pf/emergency-savings/.

3. A.L. Kennedy, "Statistics on Last Wills & Testaments," http://info.legalzoom.com/statistics-last-wills-testaments-3947.html.

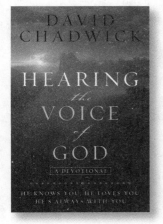

Hearing the Voice of God
David Chadwick

How do you hear the voice of God?

The answer is quite simple, yet incredibly profound. The best way to hear God's voice is through reading, studying, and meditating on his Word. As you read the Bible, you allow the Holy Spirit to speak through those words and straight into your heart.

The Gospel of John is an ideal place to start. It clearly establishes who Jesus is, his relationship with the Father, and the incredible depths of his love for you. The life-changing wisdom drawn from John will bring you into greater fellowship with God.

Each entry in this unique book begins with an assigned reading from John, followed by a key passage for the day, and concludes with an encouraging and insightful devotion. As you ponder and apply what you learn, you'll begin to hear God speaking powerfully and personally through his Word and become more attuned to his voice in all of Scripture.

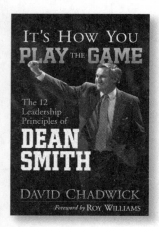

It's How You Play the Game
David Chadwick

Dean Smith won 879 games during his legendary career as a basketball coach—making him among the winningest coaches ever. He also won the respect and admiration of those who worked and played for him. What set him apart and made him so effective as a leader?

David Chadwick, who played on championship teams for Smith, provides an inside look at how Smith led and influenced others. You'll discover 12 principles that marked Smith's approach to leadership, including...

- put the team before the individual
- be flexible in your vision
- speak positive words
- make failure your friend
- commit yourself for the long haul

Whatever your calling as a leader—in business, athletics, ministry, or elsewhere—this book will equip you to play the game well...and win.

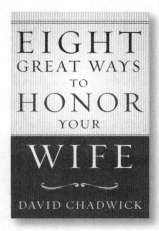

Eight Great Ways to Honor Your Wife
David Chadwick

God calls you not only to love your wife, but also to honor her. Sadly, honor is a missing ingredient in many marriages today.

Love and honor practiced together will take your marriage to a whole new level. Join author David Chadwick as he shares eight great ways to make this happen:

trust her instincts	share your heart
be a man of God	read her well
encourage her gifts	be a guardian and gardener
use words wisely	ask a certain question often

Make honoring your wife an everyday part of your life—and experience the very best of what God can do in your marriage relationship!

Eight Great Ways to Honor Your Husband
Marilynn Chadwick

When you honor your husband, you lift him up—and inspire him to become all God meant for him to be. But in today's culture, the idea of showing honor to a spouse has been all but lost. As a result, couples aren't experiencing God's best for their lives.

You can change that. In this book, author Marilynn Chadwick shares eight ways you can show this special kind of love for your husband:

become strong	guard your home
believe the best	lighten his load
build him up	dream big together
fight for him	create a culture of honor

As you honor your beloved, your relationship will rise to a whole new level—and you'll show others how beautiful a marriage can be when it follows God's design.

moments of HOPE

www.momentsofhope.org

Moments of Hope is the media ministry of David and Marilynn Chadwick.

To learn more about David and Marilynn's messages, books, radio programs, and online content, please visit momentsofhope.org.

Moments of Hope
PO Box 1163
Pineville, NC 28134

888.70(**HOPE**)4 | 888.704.6734

To learn more about Harvest House books and
to read sample chapters, log on to our website:

www.harvesthousepublishers.com

HARVEST HOUSE PUBLISHERS
EUGENE, OREGON